The Joan Palevsky  Imprint in Classical Literature

In honor of beloved Virgil—

"O degli altri poeti onore e lume . . ."

—Dante, *Inferno*

*The publisher gratefully acknowledges the generous
support of the Classical Literature Endowment Fund
of the University of California Press Foundation, which
was established by a major gift from Joan Palevsky.*

A Free Will

SATHER CLASSICAL LECTURES

Volume Sixty-eight

A Free Will

A Free Will

*Origins of the Notion
in Ancient Thought*

by Michael Frede

Edited by A. A. Long

with a Foreword by David Sedley

UNIVERSITY OF CALIFORNIA PRESS

Berkeley   Los Angeles   London

University of California Press, one of the most distinguished university presses in the United States, enriches lives around the world by advancing scholarship in the humanities, social sciences, and natural sciences. Its activities are supported by the UC Press Foundation and by philanthropic contributions from individuals and institutions. For more information, visit www.ucpress.edu.

University of California Press
Berkeley and Los Angeles, California

University of California Press, Ltd.
London, England

First paperback printing 2012

Library of Congress Cataloging-in-Publication Data

Frede, Michael.
 A free will : origins of the notion in ancient thought / edited by A. A. Long ; with a foreword by David Sedley.
    p.   cm.   —(Sather classical lectures ; v. 68)
"An edited version of the six lectures Michael Frede delivered as the 84th Sather Professor of Classical Literature at the University of California, Berkeley, in the Fall semester of 1997/98"—Pref.
 Includes bibliographical references and index.
 ISBN 978-0-520-27266-8 (pbk. : alk. paper)
 1. Free will and determinism—History.   2. Philosophy, Ancient   I. Long, A. A.
II. Title.
  B187.F7F74   2011
  123'.5093—dc22   2010020858

Manufactured in the United States of America
19 18 17 16 15 14 13 12
10 9 8 7 6 5 4 3 2 1

This book is printed on Cascades Enviro 100, a 100% post consumer waste, recycled, de-inked fiber. FSC recycled certified and processed chlorine free. It is acid free, Ecologo certified, and manufactured by BioGas energy.

CONTENTS

FOREWORD

Michael Frede's untimely death in 2007 marked off a forty-year era in the study of ancient philosophy upon which he has left his unique mark. This imprint owed much to his intellectual persona. At Göttingen (1966–71), Berkeley (1971–76), Princeton (1976–91), Oxford (1991–2005), and, in his final years, Athens (2005–2007), he was a magnet to younger scholars, many of whom have gone on to become leaders in the field. For them and others he set an inspiring example by his dialectical practice of live discussion, which, provided that it was accompanied by sufficient coffee and cigarettes, was liable to continue hour upon hour without limit. He was unfailingly supportive of his countless former students, in many of whom the spirit and style of his scholarship live on.

For the wider world, however, his writings were the primary conduit of his influence. They started with *Prädikation und Existenzaussage* (1967), his seminal monograph on Plato's *Sophist*, and continued through his superlative book on Stoic logic (1974), his celebrated commentary (coauthored by Gunther Patzig) on Aristotle, *Metaphysics* Zeta (1988), innumerable articles and chapters, three edited collections, a translation (with Richard Walzer) of *Three Treatises on the Nature of Science* by Galen, and a volume of Frede's reprinted papers (1987), to which further volumes are now to be posthumously added. The present book further enlarges, perhaps even crowns, that remarkable corpus of work.

From the twelve centuries during which Greco-Roman philosophy flourished, there are few thinkers or topics whose understanding has not been enriched by Frede's publications. A full list would be tediously long. Plato and the dialogue form; Aristotelian category theory and metaphysics; Stoic logic, grammar, ethics, and epistemology; Pyrrhonist skepticism; and Galen's theology are no more than examples of the subjects whose understanding has been permanently transformed by Frede's now classic studies. I do not mean by this that he has definitively solved the major historical or exegetical problems; his views have as often as not generated new controversy. Rather, his example and contribution have dramatically clarified the issues and raised the level of debate, introducing entirely new perspectives and interpretative options.

Frede was invited to be the eighty-fourth Sather Professor of Classical Literature at his former university, the University of California, Berkeley, in 1997–98. The professorship requires its holder to give six lectures that will later be published by the University of California Press in its Sather Classical Lectures series, which includes such celebrated works as E. R. Dodds, *The Greeks and the Irrational* (1951), and Bernard Williams, *Shame and Necessity* (1993). As Tony Long explains in his preface, although the lectures were extremely well received, Frede did not feel ready to publish them before extending his research further. But as readers will quickly discover, the quality of the text that he has bequeathed fully matches the brilliance and incisiveness for which all his work is admired.

The origin of the concept of will, and more specifically free will, has been endlessly debated, and the inconclusiveness of the debate has mirrored the philosophical indeterminacy of the concept itself. Frede's strategy is to avoid any initial presuppositions about the term's precise meaning and instead let his understanding of it emerge from the texts. This leads him to set Aristotle aside (albeit in a characteristically illuminating chapter) and to shift the focus firmly to Stoicism, arguing that it was in Epictetus that the earlier Stoic theory of assent, enriched with a now developed notion of an inner life, led to the first philosophical concept plausibly identifiable as free will. Much of Frede's past work on Stoic psychology is fruitfully redeployed in securing this result. Later chapters are devoted to showing how the underlying Stoic notion, despite not being able to commend itself in unmodified form to Platonism and Aristotelianism, was the one that ultimately found its way into Christian doctrine.

In addition to its potential to become a landmark in the historiography of philosophy, this book displays the familiar magic of Michael Frede's writing at his usual best. One of the earliest lessons he learned, he once told me, was not to dress up as complicated anything that is fundamentally simple. And that capacity for putting across a powerfully illuminating perspective without the least pretension, but with a winning combination of lucidity, patience, and penetratingly sharp vision, will be found to be on display once more in the pages that follow.

David Sedley

EDITOR'S PREFACE

This book is an edited version of the six lectures Michael Frede delivered as the eighty-fourth Sather Professor of Classical Literature at the University of California, Berkeley, during the fall semester of 1997–98. Frede entitled his lectures "The Origins of the Notion of the Will." They were well attended by the campus community and received with great interest and appreciation. The Department of Classics was eager to publish the lectures as soon as Frede was ready to commit them to print, but he insisted that, before doing so, he needed to discuss further ancient authors and related topics. This perfectionism was completely in character, but by summer 2007 we were still hoping to receive a typescript from him that we could send to the University of California Press. Then, on August 11 of that year, during a triennial colloquium on Hellenistic philosophy at Delphi, Frede died unexpectedly while swimming in the Gulf of Corinth.

What additions and changes he might have made, but for his untimely death, we shall sadly never know. In conversation with me in the years since he delivered his Sather Lectures, he spoke eagerly about his interests in Maximus the Confessor and John Chrysostomos; as this book's bibliography shows, in 2002 he published a substantial article entitled "John of Damascus on Human Action, the Will, and Human Freedom." We can be fairly confident that Byzantine philosophy and theology was the field in which he would have expanded his research on the will. But, though he himself was not ready to publish his lecture typescripts, they already form, as this book shows, a completely coherent and well-fashioned whole.

Having been fortunate to know Michael Frede for a period of thirty years, I readily agreed to edit the lectures when Katerina Iorediakonou, his partner, asked me to do so. I realized of course that the task would be daunting. Frede's command of ancient philosophy was legendary in its range and subtlety, and his Sather Lectures drew him into Patristic scholarship, where I was far from being at home. However, I knew I could count on help wherever my own familiarity with the material ran out. In compiling the notes, which were not part of the original typescript, I have consulted the following friends: Alan Code, John Dillon, Dorothea Frede, James Hankinson, James O'Donnell, and Robert Sharples. George Boys-Stones deserves special mention as he is largely responsible for the notes for chapter 7, on Origen. I am also grateful to my colleague Mark Griffith, who wrote the Sather committee's report recommending the book's publication to the University of California Press and gave me several suggestions and corrections that I have gladly incorporated.

As Frede indicated in his first lecture (chapter 1), he conceived his project, to quite a large extent, as a response to the Sather Lectures delivered by his compatriot, Albrecht Dihle, in 1974 and published in 1982 under the title *The Theory of Will in Classical Antiquity*. Frede fully acknowledges Dihle's extraordinary learning, but he contests his predecessor's thesis that the effective originator of the notion of a free will was Augustine. According to Frede, it is later Stoicism, as represented by Epictetus, that was chiefly responsible for developing the notion of a free will, with Augustine himself one of the chief beneficiaries of this Stoic notion.

Frede entitled his lectures, as I have mentioned, "The Origins of the Notion of the Will." In fact, as he makes plain in the introduction to this book, what chiefly concerns him are the origins of the notion of a *free* will. In editing his work I decided that it would be much more appropriately publicized by stating "free will" in the book's title rather than simply "will." I have also converted the first three chapters of his typescript, which were lengthy and closely packed, into the first six chapters of this book. Chapters 1, 3, and 5 retain Frede's original lecture titles, as do chapters 7 to 9. But chapters 2, 4, and 6, with titles I have invented, incorporate material Frede included in the second half of each of his typescript chapters 1, 2, and 3.

In editing the material I have been chiefly concerned to smooth the flow of sentences and paragraphs in ways that still respect the inimitable tone of Frede's voice. In a few instances I was not sure of his meaning, and I have indicated these in the notes. Most often the changes I have introduced are to punctuation, syntax, and word order, pruning some of the profuse uses of *now* or *and* at the beginning of sentences and eliminating repetition that works better in a lecture than in a text for reading. I have also introduced a few subheadings or white space between paragraphs, in order to temper the density of some passages. I was greatly helped with the mechanics of editing by Nandini Pandey, a graduate student at Berkeley, who put the preliminarily edited typescript on line and spotted many necessary changes that I had overlooked. I am also grateful to David Crane, another Berkeley graduate student, who read parts of the typescript with me at an early stage and made helpful editorial suggestions.

In most of his publications Frede was sparing in the use of notes and in references to scholarly literature. This book departs somewhat from that practice, but I have been encouraged by friends, among whom I am especially grateful to Charles Brittain, to annotate Frede's text to the extent that I have done. His work is of such high quality and of such general interest that it deserves a large readership. I have compiled the book's notes and bibliography, modest in scope and quantity though they are, in the hope that they will be of help to readers who are relatively new to this material and keen to pursue it further, as Frede himself would have wished .

AAL

CHAPTER ONE

Introduction

The notion of a free will is a notion we have inherited from
antiquity. It was first in antiquity that one came to think of
human beings as having a free will. But, as with so many other
notions we have inherited from antiquity, for instance, the notion
of an essence or the notion of a teleological cause, we have to
ask ourselves whether the notion of a free will has not outlived
its usefulness, has not become a burden rather than of any real
help in understanding ourselves and what we do. Contemporary
philosophers for the most part dispense with the notion of a
free will, and the few attempts which are still made to give an
account of what it is to have free will seem rather discouraging.
In this situation it may be of some help to retrace our steps and
see what purpose the notion of a free will originally was supposed to serve, how it was supposed to help our understanding,
and whether it was flawed right from its beginnings, as we might
now see in hindsight.

In these lectures it is in this spirit that I want to pursue the
question "When in antiquity did one first think of human beings

as having a free will, why did one come to think so, and what notion of a free will was involved when one came to think of human beings in this way?" To raise this question, though, is to make a substantial assumption about the very nature of the notion of a free will. I assume, and I will try to show, that this notion in its origins is a technical, philosophical notion which already presupposes quite definite and far from trivial assumptions about ourselves and the world. It is for this reason that I presume its having an identifiable historical origin.

In contrast, this is not the view scholars took until fairly recently. They went on the assumption that the notion of a free will is an ordinary notion, part of the repertory of notions in terms of which the ordinary person thinks about things and in terms of which the ancient Greeks must have already been thinking all along. And on this assumption, of course, there is no place for the question of when the ancients first came to think of human beings as having a free will.

The assumption that the Greeks all along must have been thinking of human beings as having a free will seems truly astounding nowadays. For, if we look at Greek literature from Homer onwards, down to long after Aristotle, we do not find any trace of a reference to, let alone a mention of, a free will. This is all the more remarkable, as Plato and in particular Aristotle had plenty of occasion to refer to a free will. But there is no sign of such a reference in their works. Scholars did indeed notice this with a certain amount of puzzlement. But it did not occur to them to draw what would seem to be the obvious inference, namely, that Plato and Aristotle did not yet have a notion of a free will and that it was for this reason that they did not talk of a free will. As eminent a scholar as W. D. Ross again could note that Plato and Aristotle do not refer to a will, let alone a free will.

But even Ross concludes that we must assume that Aristotle, as Ross puts it, "shared the plain man's belief in free will."[1] And he explains Aristotle's failure to refer to a free will explicitly as due to the fact that Aristotle did not think hard and carefully enough about the matter to arrive at a philosophical account of what it is to have a free will.

But why should we assume in the first place that Aristotle believed in a free will? To understand the assumption Ross and earlier scholars make, we have to take into account the following. Let us assume that it is a fact that, at least sometimes when we do something, we are responsible for what we are doing, as nothing or nobody forces us to act in this way; rather, we ourselves desire or even choose or decide to act in this way. Let us also assume, as is reasonable enough, that this is what the Greeks believed all along. It certainly is something Aristotle took to be a fact. The notion of a free will was originally introduced within the context of a particular theory, namely, a late Stoic theory, in a way specific to this theory, to account for this presumed fact. But once this notion had been introduced into Stoicism, rival theories, either Peripatetic or Platonist, developed their own version of a notion of a free will, which fitted in with their overall theory. In fact, it was a notion which was eagerly taken up by Christians, too. And, largely due to the influence of mainstream Christianity, it came to be a notion which, in one version or another, gained almost universal acceptance. People quite generally, whether followers of Stoicism, Platonism, or mainstream Christianity, felt committed to a belief in a free will. Even if they themselves were not able to give a theoretical account of what a free will is, they relied on such an account's being available. This had the effect that the mere assumption that sometimes we are responsible for what we are doing, since we do it not because we are forced to but because we ourselves want to, came to be regarded as tantamount to a belief in a free will. From here it was just a short step to the assumption that the mere notion of a free will was an ordinary notion, with philosophical theory coming in only to give a theoretical account of what it is to have a free will. This is why Ross could assume that Aristotle shared the plain man's belief in a free will but failed to give a theoretical account of that.

It seems to me to be clear, though, that we should carefully distinguish between the belief in a free will and the ordinary belief that at least sometimes we are responsible for what we are doing, because we are not forced or made to behave in this way but really want or even choose or decide to act in this way. This belief in a free will is involved in some theoretical accounts of what we ordinarily believe. But it is not to be identified with this ordinary belief. And it seems to me that Aristotle is a good example of a philosopher who is committed to the ordinary belief but does not resort to the notion of a free will to account for this belief. Hence, since even Aristotle does not yet talk of a free will, we should assume that he did not yet have a notion of a free will.

This indeed is what scholars nowadays are generally agreed on. The change of scholarly opinion is largely due to the fact that philosophical discussions, of the kind we find, for instance, in Gilbert Ryle's *The Concept of Mind,* have persuaded scholars that the notion of a free will is at best a highly controversial notion.[2] In light of this, Aristotle's failure to refer to a free will is no longer regarded as a cause for puzzlement but by many is registered with outright relief.

Once one finally comes to see that it is not the case that the Greeks all along had a notion of a free will and that we do not yet find this notion even in Aristotle, the question naturally poses itself: When did the notion of a free will arise? And so more recent scholars have begun to inquire into this question.

By far the most substantial attempt to answer this question was made by Albrecht Dihle in his Sather Lectures of 1974, which were published by the University of California Press in 1982 under the title *The Theory of Will in Classical Antiquity.* This book remains the most important contribution to the subject. One must admire the wide learning and insight which went into its writing. But, even if one does not dispose of the kind of learning Dihle does, one cannot help being struck by one fact about his account which pervasively shapes his book. It is an account which is focused on a highly specific notion of a free will. What Dihle attempts to lay bare and to shed light on is the origin of this particular notion of a free will. He calls it "our modern notion of will."[3] This cannot fail to provoke two reactions.

To begin with, we should query the phrase, "our modern notion of will," especially since Dihle assumes that this notion of will is a notion of a free will.[4] In light of what we have said before, he hardly seems entitled to the assumption that there is one notion of a will, and a free will at that, which we all share. Dihle talks as if a certain notion of the will, though not there all along, became common currency from a certain point onwards up to the present. But this does not seem to be true. He is of course perfectly entitled to a view about how we all should or would conceive of the will, if we had properly understood what a will is. But, if we then look more closely at what Dihle has to say about the will, it turns out to be a notion of a free will which is dangerously close to the kind of notion which philosophers have been attacking, a notion which is supposed to do justice to the presumed fact that we can do something by sheer volition, by a sheer act of the will.

Second, the very phrase "our modern notion of will" quite rightly reminds us that history presents us with a wide variety of versions of a notion of a free will, which differ quite substantially from Dihle's favored notion, presumed to be our notion. In part these differ in that, as he puts it, they are much too "intellectualistic" and not "voluntaristic" enough.[5] Dihle passes over all such notions with little or no discussion, as they cannot count as notions of a will in what he takes to be our sense of the concept.

It seems to me that Dihle does indeed contribute a great deal to our understanding of the historical origins of a specific notion of a free will—one that is still quite widespread and that many may think captures the way we ought to conceive of the will as such. But my aim is completely different from Dihle's. I do not aim to elucidate the origins of some specific notion of a free will which we might have, let alone a notion I myself favor. For I regard my inquiry as purely historical. I do not want it to depend on, and be shaped and slanted by, a notion of a free will which at best can be regarded as philosophically quite controversial. Rather, I am interested, as I said at the outset, in trying to find out when and why a notion of a free will arose in the first place and what notion this was. I will then try to trace the history of this notion to see whether and how it changed in the course of the discussions to which it gave rise in antiquity. In this way, I hope, we shall also be able to identify the ancestor of Dihle's favored notion of a free will or, for that matter, the ancestors of any later notion of a free will. It is in this sense that I plan to talk about the origins of the notion of a free will.

Now, though I do not presuppose a specific notion of a free will, let alone want to endorse or advocate some specific notion of it, I do rely on something like a general idea of a free will, something like a schema which any specific notion of a free will or any particular version of the notion of a free will, at least in antiquity, will fit into. I do not arrive at this general idea or schema on the basis of some philosophical view as to what any notion of a free will has to look like but rather with the benefit of historical hindsight. That is to say, I have looked at the relevant ancient texts and have abstracted this schema from those texts which explicitly talk of a will, the freedom of the will, or a free will. In having such a schema, we shall at least have a general idea of what we are looking for when we investigate the origins of the notion of a free will but without having to commit ourselves to any particular view, ancient or modern, as to what a free will really is.

It should be clear that in order to have any such notion, one must first of all have a notion of a will. As a matter of historical fact, it turns out that a notion of a will is not necessarily a notion of a will which is free. In any case, in order to have a notion of a free will, one must, in addition to the notion of a will, also have a notion of freedom. These notions of a will and of freedom must be such that it makes sense to say that we have a will which is free.

In order to get any notion of a will at all, one must assume the following. Unless one is literally forced or made to do something in such a manner that what one is doing is in no way one's own action (as when one is pushing something over because one is pushed oneself), one does what one does because something happens in one's mind which makes one do what one does. Moreover, one has to assume that what happens in one's mind which makes one do what one does is that one chooses or decides to act in this way. Or at least one has to assume that there is something going on in the mind which can be construed as a choice or decision. We need not worry for the moment about this qualification or its significance. Thus, for instance, if one feels hungry or feels like having something to eat, one might or might not choose or decide to have something to eat. If one then does have something to eat, it is because one has chosen or decided to have something to eat, since one feels hungry.

But the notion of the will, at least in antiquity, involves a notion of the mind such that the mere fact that one feels hungry will not yet explain why one is having something to eat. This is supposed to be so, because, even if one does feel hungry or does feel like having something to eat, one might choose or decide not to have anything to eat because one thinks that it would not be a good thing to have something to eat now. One might also decide to have something to eat, though one does not feel hungry at all, because one thinks that it would be a good thing to have something to eat. But, in any case, for there to be an action that is one's own action, there is supposed to be an event in one's mind, a mental act, a choice or decision which brings about the action. The notion of a will, then, is the notion of our ability to make such choices or decisions which make us act in the way we do. It is crucial for the notion of the will that this ability differs greatly from person to person, as different people not only have different thoughts about what is or is not a good thing to do but also have quite different feelings about different things. This is why different people in the same situation will make very different choices and hence will act quite differently. It is also crucial for the notion of the will that it is an ability which needs to be developed, cultivated, and perfected. One can get better and better at making choices, just as one can get worse and worse. One can choose or decide to improve one's will, one's ability to make choices.

The standard Greek term for the will is *prohairesis,* literally, "choice" or "disposition to choose." Later *boulēsis* and, in particular, *thelēsis* will also be used in this sense, especially in Byzantine times. The standard Latin term, of course, is *voluntas.* The Greek term for the relevant notion of freedom is *eleutheria.* This term provides us with some guidance as to how the notion of freedom we are interested in is to be understood. As the very term indicates, it must be a notion formed by analogy to the political notion of freedom. According to the political notion, one is free if one is a citizen rather than a slave and living in a free political community rather than in a community governed, for instance, by a tyrant. This political notion of freedom is two-sided. It is characterized, on the one side, by the laws which the citizens of the community have imposed on themselves and, on the other side, by there being no further external constraints on a free citizen which would systematically prevent him from doing what he could reasonably want to do in pursuit of his own good, in particular from living the kind of life he could reasonably want to live. It is crucial that this freedom, to put the matter in a grossly simplified form, almost invariably seems to be understood as a freedom from external constraints which go beyond the acceptable constraints involved in living in a political community and which would systematically prevent one from doing what it takes to have a good life. Living under a tyrant and being a slave are regarded as involving such constraints, as the tyrant and the slave master, by definition, impose constraints on what one can do which systematically prevent one from having a good life, at least given a certain traditional understanding of what a good life amounts to.

The notion of freedom we are interested in is formed by analogy to this political notion, but its precise relation to the political is never definitively settled, in good part for political and social reasons; being formed by analogy to the political notion, it also inherits its double-sided character. Thus the ability of a free person to have a good life is understood more precisely as the ability to live a good life in what we, not very helpfully, might be tempted to call a moral sense. The lack of clarity about the relation between the political notion and this personal notion of freedom in part is due to a lack of clarity about the relation between the good life one is able to have when one is politically free and the good life one can live if one has personal freedom. The tendency among ancient philosophers, needless to say, is to claim that one can live a good life even under a tyrant or as a slave.

What, then, are the external constraints which this personal notion of freedom envisages which could systematically prevent us from doing what we need to do in order to live a good life, assuming that the constraints a tyrant or a slave master could impose on us do not count as such? The answer, in a nutshell and again very grossly simplified, is that at the time when the notion of a free will arises, there are any number of views, some of them widespread, according to which the world we live in, or at least part of the world we live in, is run by a tyrant or a slave master or a whole group of them. We should not forget that even Christians like Augustine or John of Damascus had no difficulty in thinking that the right way to characterize our relationship to God is to say that we are slaves of God. Now the Christian God is a benevolent agent who provides for his slaves in such a way as to enable them to live a good life. Even on this view there is an obvious tension between our being free and our being slaves, one may even say at least an apparent contradiction. But there were lots of other views, according to which those who rule the world, or our sublunary part of it, are far from benevolent, far from concerned about our well-being.

There are, for instance, the so-called *archontes*, the rulers or planetary gods who rule the sublunary world and determine what happens in it, including our lives, so as to fit their designs and ideas and to serve their interests as they perceive them.[6] They do not care about what this does to our lives or to our ability to have or to live a good life. Indeed, they might try to do what they can to make it impossible for us to live a good life. There is also a widespread view, which we find among groups (following some early Christian authors like Irenaeus) we have come to call "Gnostics," according to which the agent who created the visible world we live in, the demiurge or creator, is a being which pursues its own interests without regard for what this does to us, a being lacking in wisdom and goodness, as one can see from the fact that it deludes itself into thinking that it is God and demanding worship. This view, if held by Gnostics, as a rule seems to be combined with the view that this God is the God of Jewish scripture, who created this world which in all sorts of ways reflects his lack of wisdom and goodness, for instance, in that it puts at least many, if not all of us, into a position in which it is impossible to live a good life.

It is against the background of a large number of such views that the notion of freedom we are interested in emerges. To say that human beings are free is to say that the world does not put such constraints on us from the outside as to make it impossible for us to live a good life. These views will strike most of us as extremely fanciful. But we should keep in mind that late antiquity was full of such views, which exercised an enormous attraction. And we should also keep in mind that there were other views which, though much less fanciful, were also perceived to put at least into question whether we are free.

The views in question assume some kind of physical determinism, according to which everything which happens, including our actions, is determined by antecedent physical causes and is thus predetermined. The nearest we ever get in antiquity to the kind of physical determinism we are now thinking of, when we talk about determinism, is in Epicurus, if only for Epicurus to reject it without much of an argument.[7] Epicurus is concerned that the kind of atomism introduced by Democritus, and espoused by himself, might be misunderstood as entailing a view according to which everything which happens, including what we do, is predetermined by an endless chain of antecedent causes. If this were true, nothing that we do would in any substantial sense depend on us. For the conditions from which it would ineluctably follow that one day you would exist, that you would be this sort of person with those beliefs and those desires, and that in a certain situation you would respond to this situation in this way, would already be there all along. These conditions would have come about without any thought of you, without any regard to you or your life, and you certainly would have had no active part in bringing them about. So your action would just be a part of how the world ineluctably unfolds from antecedent conditions which have predetermined your action long before you existed.

It is almost impossible for us not to understand Democritus in the way Epicurus rejects. Democritus assumes that all there is are atoms moving in a void. They collide and rebound, form transient compounds, among them compounds which are relatively stable, owing to the configuration of their constituent atoms. What we call "objects," including plants, animals, and human beings, are such compounds. These entities, owing to the particular configurations of their constituent atoms, display a certain regularity in their behavior.

We can hardly resist the temptation to assume wrongly that Democritus must have thought that the atoms move, collide, or rebound according to fixed laws of nature, such that everything which happens ultimately is governed by these laws. But it is perfectly clear that Democritus has no idea of such laws. He is concerned, rather, to resist the idea that the apparent regularity in the behavior of objects be understood as the result of their being designed to behave in this fashion; for in Greek thought regularity of behavior as a rule is associated with design by an intellect. The planets are taken to be supremely intelligent, if not wise, because they move with an extreme degree of regularity.[8] If an object is not intelligent but displays regularity in behavior, it is readily thought to do so by design of an intelligent agent. Democritus's point is that the apparent regularity in the world is not a work of design, say, by an Anaxagorean cosmic intellect but a surface phenomenon produced by the aimless, random motion of the atoms. Thus apparent regularity is supposed to be explained in terms of randomness. But already in Epicurus's day there was the temptation to think of the motion of the atoms as itself regular. Hence Epicurus, to avoid this misinterpretation of his own atomism, tries to insist on the irregularity of the motion of the atoms by claiming that they swerve from their paths without cause.[9]

Epicurus's doctrine of the swerve, it seems to me, has been widely misunderstood as a doctrine which is meant to explain human freedom, as if a postulated swerve of atoms in the mind could explain such a thing. Epicurus's point is, rather, that, since the world is not deterministic in this way, it does not constitute a threat to the idea that some of the things we do are genuinely our own actions, rather than something which happens to us or something we are made to do. But here is at least an envisaged possible view, which is not fanciful at all but is rather close to what we call physical determinism. According to that, the world puts constraints on what we can do, which are such that we cannot but do whatever it is that we are doing, and hence might systematically prevent us from doing what we would need to do to live a good life.

The doctrine which in antiquity comes nearest to physical determinism in our sense, and was actually espoused, is the Stoic doctrine of fate.[10] According to the Stoics, everything which happens has antecedent physical causes which form a chain reaching back as far as we care to trace it. But even this form of universal physical determinism differs radically from its modern counterpart in three crucial respects. First, Stoic fate is the work of an agent, namely, God, whose plan dictates the way the world evolves and changes, including what we ourselves do, down to the smallest detail.[11] Modern determinists, in contrast, do not normally believe in a cosmic agent who determines things. Second, this plan is providential precisely in the sense that the Stoic God predetermines things in part with regard to us, taking into consideration what his determination does to us and to our life. Modern determinists, however, will find it natural to think not only that everything we do is predetermined but also that our choices and decisions are predetermined entirely without regard to us. Third, in a curious twist to the Stoic position (and with nothing comparable in the case of modern determinism), the divine plan itself seems to be contingent on our choices and decisions, in such a way that God anticipates them in determining the way the world evolves.

In any case, God in his providence sets the world up in such a way that there are no constraints imposed on us from the outside which would systematically make it impossible for us to do what we need to do to live a good life. So here we do have a form of causal determinism, but it was a matter of dispute whether it posed a threat to freedom or not. Tellingly, those who argued that it did, like Alexander of Aphrodisias, conveniently disregarded the idea that, on this theory, our choices are not just the product of fate but themselves to some extent determine fate.[12]

Universal causal determinism, though, was not a view which had many adherents in antiquity. This was not because the ancients believed for the most part that things happen without a cause or an explanation. For the most part they came to believe that things do have a natural cause or explanation. But they had a very different conception from ours of what constitutes a cause or explanation. Perhaps the most crucial difference is that nobody in antiquity had the notion of laws of nature, meaning a body of laws which govern and explain the behavior of all objects, irrespective of their kind. For the most part, at least, philosophers believed (and this is true, though in different ways, of Aristotelians, Platonists, Stoics, and Epicureans alike) that the most important factor for one's understanding of the way things behave is the nature of an object. If you wish, you can think of the nature of an object as something which could be explained by a set of principles and laws which govern and explain the behavior of objects with this nature, for instance, plants or stars. But they are principles and laws governing a specific set of items. The nature of an object puts certain internal constraints on what objects of this kind or nature can do. Human beings, for instance, cannot do everything; just because they are human beings, they cannot fly, even if they wanted to. But there are also lots of things the nature of an object enables it to do. For instance, the nature of a sunflower enables it to turn in the direction of the sun. In fact, it makes the flower turn towards the sun, when the sun is visible. Quite generally, the nature of an object is such that, given certain specifiable conditions, it cannot but behave in a certain identifiable way.

It is only when we come to more complex animals and, of course, to human beings that the behavior is not entirely determined by the nature of the object and the circumstances or conditions the object finds itself in. Animals can learn, be trained, or even be taught to do certain things. Different animals of the same kind might behave quite differently in the same circumstances. Their behavior is not entirely fixed by their nature or the laws of their nature. And, notoriously, human beings have to be trained and taught and educated. They have to learn a lot before they are able to act in a truly human and mature way. What is more, and what is crucially important, human beings have to actively involve themselves in acquiring the competence it takes to lead a truly human life. It is certainly not by their nature that human beings act virtuously.

Given a view of the world in which what happens is largely accounted for in terms of the nature of things, there may be nothing which does not have a natural cause and explanation, but, given the kinds of causes and explanations appealed to, the world might remain in our sense causally underdetermined, leaving enough space for us to live our life as we see fit. But, as we come to late antiquity, there is a growing sense that at least the physical world may be determined. Yet by then, of course, there is also the view, which rapidly spreads, that the mind is not physical. In any case, the notion of freedom gets its point only from the fact that there are available at the time numerous views about the world, according to which we are under such constraints as to possibly, if not necessarily, be unable to do what we need to do to live a good life.

With this we come to the combination of the two notions of

the will, on the one hand, and of freedom, on the other hand, in the notion of a free will. Given the view that our actions are caused by a choice or a decision of the will, our freedom to do the things we need to do in order to live a good life must involve the freedom to make the choices which need to be made in order to produce the actions which need to be taken. This, however, is a trivial connection between the will and freedom. It would hardly explain the great emphasis on the freedom of the will.

A less trivial connection is this. We might act under such constraints that the choices we have are so limited that they might not produce a good life. Just think of a cosmic tyrant who again and again confronts you with a choice like this: having your children killed or betraying your friends; or killing your child or being condemned for not obeying the order to kill your child. This too, though, would hardly suffice to explain the emphasis on freedom of the will.

A still more promising connection is this. As soon as we think of a world run by a cosmic tyrant—or by planetary intellects and their daemonic minions who have access to our mind, perhaps can manipulate it, and perhaps can systematically try to prevent us from gaining the knowledge we would need to live a good life—we can see that there is a special point in emphasizing the freedom of the will. No cosmic power has such a force over our minds as to prevent the will from making the choices it needs to make.

There is, though, yet a further connection. By the time we come to late antiquity, most people think that in one important sense our freedom is reduced to the freedom of the mind and in particular the will. For, even if we choose to act in a certain way, we have no control over whether we shall succeed in doing out there in the world what we decided to do in our mind. We may decide to cross the street but be run over as we try to do so. We may decide to raise our arm, but the arm does not rise. The doctrine of a free will is certainly not a doctrine to explain how we manage to raise our arm or cross the street. It is, rather, a doctrine of how we are responsible for raising our arm, if we do raise our arm, irrespective of the fact that the world out there is populated by agents of various kinds who might thwart our endeavor.[13] At least for Stoics, Christians, and, to a lesser degree, Platonists, there is also divine providence, which already has settled ab initio whether what we decide to do fits into its plan for the best possible world and hence will be allowed to come to fruition.

This, then, is the general schema for a notion of a free will. Our next major step will be to see how the notion of a specific and actual will first emerged in Stoicism. But before we can turn to this, we have to take a look at Aristotle.

CHAPTER TWO

Aristotle on Choice without a Will

There are at least three reasons why we should begin our detailed study with Aristotle. First, the Stoics can only develop a notion of a will, because they have a certain notion of the mind. But they have developed this notion of the mind in opposition to Plato's and Aristotle's notion of the mind, or rather of the soul. Second, we should reassure ourselves that we have understood not only that Aristotle does not have a notion of a free will but also why he does not have a notion of a free will. Third, there will come a time in late antiquity when Aristotle is studied again with great care by philosophers and when at least some of his writings are recommended, if not required, reading for any highly educated person. What we find as a result, if we look at certain philosophical authors—but also at some influential Christian writers like Nemesius of Emesa—is that they reimport into a discussion, which by this point has moved far beyond Aristotle, certain doctrines from the *Nicomachean Ethics* in a way that confused, rather than clarified, matters.

Neither Plato nor Aristotle has a notion of a will. What they do have, though, is a closely related notion, namely, the notion of somebody's willing or wanting something, in particular, somebody's willing or wanting to do something, the notion of *boulesthai* or of a *boulēsis.* Indeed, this notion plays a fundamental role in their thought about human beings and their behavior, and it will continue to play a crucial role throughout antiquity. But the term *boulesthai* will be a source of confusion, and hence it is important to be clear about what it means in Plato and in Aristotle. It will be a source of confusion in part because the word is the Greek version of a verb which we seem to find in many, if not all, Indo-European languages, for example, *velle* in Latin and its derivatives in the Romance languages, and *wollen* in German, or "to will" in English. These languages also form a corresponding noun, like *voluntas* in Latin, or "will" in English, which from a certain point onwards will also be used to refer to the will, though the Greeks are rather late and hesitant in using *boulēsis* in this way.

Yet the intimate etymological connection should not confuse us into thinking that *boulesthai,* at least as used in Plato and Aristotle and in later Greek philosophy, has the same rather broad use as Latin *velle* or German *wollen* or English "to will" in the sense of "to want." In Plato and Aristotle it refers to a highly specific form of wanting or desiring, in fact, a form of wanting which we no longer recognize or for which we tend to have no place in our conceptual scheme. For Plato and Aristotle willing, as I will call it, is a form of desire which is specific to reason.[1] It is the form in which reason desires something. If reason recognizes, or believes itself to recognize, something as a good, it wills or desires it. If reason believes itself to see a course of action which would allow us to attain this presumed good, it thinks that it is a good thing, other things being equal, to take this course of action. And, if it thinks that it is a good thing to do something, it wills or desires to do it. Thus it is assumed that there is such a thing as a desire of reason and hence also that reason by itself suffices to motivate us to do something. This is an assumption which is made by Socrates, Plato, Aristotle, the Stoics, and their later followers. They all agree that reason, just as it is attracted by truth, is also attracted by, and attached to, the good and tries to attain it.

In Plato and Aristotle but not in the Stoics, this view of willing, as a form of desire distinctive of reason, is closely bound up with the view that the soul is bipartite or, rather, tripartite, meaning that, in addition to reason, it consists of a nonrational part or parts. (I will, for our purposes, disregard their specification of two nonrational parts.) This division of the soul is based on the assumption that there are radically different forms of desire, and correspondingly radically different forms of motivation, which may even be in conflict with each other and which therefore must have their origin in different capacities, abilities, or parts of the soul.[2] Thus one may be hungry, and in this way desire something to eat, and hence desire to get something to eat. This sort of desire is called *appetite (epithymia)*. It is clearly a nonrational desire. One may be hungry, no matter what one thinks or believes. One may be hungry, even though one believes that it would not be a good thing at all to have something to eat. One might be right in believing this. Hence a nonrational desire may be a reasonable or an unreasonable desire. Similarly, though, it might be quite unreasonable for one to believe that it would be a good thing to have something to eat. Hence a desire of reason too might be a reasonable or an unreasonable desire. Therefore the distinction between reasonable and unreasonable desires is not the same as the distinction between desires of reason, or rational desires, and desires of the nonrational part of the soul, or nonrational desires. It is also assumed that, just as one may act on a rational desire, one may act on a nonrational desire. What is more, one may do so, even if this nonrational desire is in conflict with a rational desire.

Now, the assumption that, if there is a conflict, one may follow either reason or appetite amounts, of course, to a denial of Socrates' claim that nobody ever acts against his better knowledge or, indeed, against his mere beliefs. So, according to Socrates, if you really believe, whether rightly or wrongly, that it is not a good thing to have something to eat now, you will not be driven by appetite, as if your reason were a slave dragged around by the passions, and have something to eat.[3] Plato's and Aristotle's doctrine of a tripartite soul and different forms of motivation, with their possible conflict and the resolution of such conflict, constitutes an attempt to correct Socrates' position, in order to do justice to the presumed fact that people sometimes, in cases of conflict, do act, against their better knowledge, on their nonrational desire. In any event, Aristotle in his famous discussion of this presumed phenomenon, called *akrasia,* or, rather misleadingly, "weakness of will," is explicitly attacking Socrates' position.[4] Now, in looking at this discussion in the *Nicomachean Ethics,* it is important to notice that it is not focused, as modern readers apparently can hardly help thinking, on cases of acute mental conflict, that is to say, on cases in which we sit there anguished, tormented, torn apart by two conflicting desires which pull us in opposite directions, while we try to make up our mind which direction to take. We tend to read Aristotle in this way, because we have a certain conception of the mind which we project onto Aristotle. But the cases on which Aristotle is focusing are rather different.

Take the case of impetuous *akrasia.* Somebody insults you,

and you get so upset and angry that you let your anger preempt any thought you would have, if you took time to think about an appropriate response. You just act on your anger. Once you have calmed down, you might realize that you do not think that this is an appropriate way to respond to the situation. In general, you think that this is not a good way to act. But at the time you act, you have no such thought. The conflict here is a conflict between a nonrational desire and a rational desire which you would have, if you gave yourself or had the space to think about it. Or look at the very different case of *akrasia* of appetite. You have the rational desire not to eat any sweets. At some point you decided not to have any sweets. But now a delicious sweet is offered to you, and your appetite may be such that, at least for the moment, it does not even come into your mind that you do not want to eat sweets any more. This again is not a case of acute conflict. But, whichever cases of *akrasia* we consider, Aristotle's view is never that, if we are confronted with such a conflict, whether it is acute or not, and act on a nonrational desire against reason, we do so because there is a mental event, namely, a choice or a decision to act in this way. And certainly it is not the case that one chooses or decides between acting on one's belief and acting on one's nonrational desire. For, as we have seen, the way Aristotle describes these cases, they often, if not for the most part, do not even involve an occurrent thought to the effect that it would not be a good thing to act in this way.

More important, Aristotle himself explicitly characterizes these cases as ones in which one acts against one's choice *(pro-hairesis)*, rather than as cases in which one chooses to act against reason.[5] What in Aristotle's view explains that one is acting against one's own beliefs is not a choice which causes the action. It is, rather, a long story about how in the past one has failed to submit oneself to the training, practice, exercise, discipline, and reflection which would ensure that one's nonrational desires are reasonable, that one acts for reasons, rather than on impulse, and hence that, if there is a conflict, one follows reason. It is this past failure, rather than a specific mental event, a choice or decision, which in Aristotle accounts for *akratic* action.

It should now be clear why Aristotle does not have a notion of a will. One's willing, one's desire of reason, is a direct function of one's cognitive state, of what reason takes to be a good thing to do. One's nonrational desire is a direct function of the state of the nonrational part of the soul. One acts either on a rational desire, a willing, or on a nonrational desire, an appetite. In the case of conflict, there is not a further instance which would adjudicate or resolve the matter. In particular, reason is not made to appear in two roles, first as presenting its own case and then as adjudicating the conflict by making a decision or choice. How the conflict gets resolved is a matter of what happened in the past, perhaps the distant past.

What Aristotle does have is a distinction between things we do *hekontes* and things we do *akontes*.[6] The distinction he is aiming at is the distinction between things we do for which we can be held responsible and things we do for which we cannot be held responsible. Aristotle tries to draw the distinction by marking off things we do only because we are literally forced to do them or because we act out of ignorance, that is to say, because we are not aware, and could not possibly be expected to be aware, of a crucial feature of the situation, such that, if we had been aware of it, we would have acted otherwise. If somebody offers you a chocolate, he might not be aware, and there may have been no way for him to know, a crucial fact involved, namely, that the chocolate is poisoned, such that, if he had known this, he would not have offered it to you. We are, then, responsible for those things we do which we do neither by force nor out of ignorance. Put positively, for us to be responsible for what we do, our action has to somehow reflect our motivation. We must have acted in this way, because in one way or another we were motivated to act in this way, that is, either by a rational desire or a nonrational desire or both.

Traditionally, and highly misleadingly, Aristotle's distinction is represented as the distinction between the voluntary and the involuntary, and Aristotle's terms *hekōn* and *akōn* are translated accordingly. This tradition is ancient. Already Cicero translates *hekōn* in this way.[7] It reflects a projection of a later conception of the mind onto Aristotle. To begin with, we have to keep in mind that Aristotle's distinction is supposed to apply to all beings—for instance, domestic animals, children, and mature human beings—who have been trained or taught or have learned to behave in a certain way and whom we can therefore expect to behave in a certain way. If we hold an animal responsible, scold and punish it to discourage it or praise and reward it to encourage it, we do so not because we think that it made the right choice or that it had any choice. At least Aristotle assumes that the animal, whatever it does, just acts on a nonrational desire, albeit one which may be the product of conditioning and habituation, which may or may not have been fully successful. The same, more or less, according to Aristotle, is true of children. But children begin to have and act on rational desires, and mature human beings should have, and should act on, rational desires rather than on impulse. But when they nevertheless do act on a nonrational desire, again it is not by choice. The nonrational desire in and by itself suffices to motivate us, even when we are grown up. And, as we have seen, even if we act against our rational desire, this does not involve a choice. Thus there is no notion of a will, or a willing, in Aristotle, such that somebody could be said to act voluntarily or willingly, whether he acts on a rational or a nonrational desire. Hence for Aristotle responsibility also does not involve a will, since any form of motivation to act in a given way suffices for responsibility.[8]

But, as I have already indicated, this does not mean that Aristotle does not have a notion of choice. For he says that if one acts on a nonrational desire against one's better knowledge, one acts against one's choice. Indeed, the notion of a choice plays an important role in Aristotle.[9] For he thinks that if an action is to count as a virtuous action, it has to satisfy a number of increasingly strict conditions. It must not only be the right thing to do, one must be doing it *hekōn,* of one's own accord; indeed, one must will to do it. What is more, one must do it from choice *(ek prohaireseōs),* that is, one must choose *(prohaireisthai)* to do it, and the choice itself must satisfy certain conditions. Hence Aristotle explains what it is to choose to do something. In doing so, given what we have said, he also distinguishes choosing from willing. This has contributed to a widespread misunderstanding of what Aristotle takes choosing to be. It is often thought that willing and choosing are two entirely different things, that choice is a composite desire, consisting of a nonrational desire to do something and a belief, arrived at by deliberation, that it would be a good thing to act in this way in this situation.

I hardly need point out that this interpretation in part is driven by a model of the mind according to which our actions are determined by our beliefs and our nonrational desires, and in any case are motivated by our nonrational desires. But this clearly is not Aristotle's view, given his notion of willing. The reason why he distinguishes willing and choosing is not that willing and choosing are altogether different but that choosing is a very special form of willing. One may will or want something which is unattainable. One may will to do something which one is unable to do. One may will something without having any idea as to what one should do to attain it. Choosing is different. We can choose to do something only if, as Aristotle puts it, it is up to us *(eph' hēmin)*, if it is in our hands, if whether it gets done or not or happens or not depends on us.[10] Thus one cannot choose to be elected to an office, since whether one is elected depends on others. But one can will or want to be elected to an office.

Yet choosing still is a form of willing. In Aristotle's view there is a certain good which we all will or want to attain in life, namely, a good life. As grown-up human beings, we have a certain conception, though different people have rather different ones, of what this final good consists of. So in a particular situation we shall, as mature human beings, choose what to do in light of our conception of this final good, because we think, having deliberated about the matter, that acting in this way will help us to attain this good. But this is what willing to do something is: desiring to do something, because one thinks that it will help one to attain something which one considers a good and which one therefore wills or wants. Hence choosing is just a special form of willing. So in Aristotle's account choice does play an important role. But choices are not explained in terms of a will but in terms of the attachment of reason to the good, however it might be conceived of, and the exercise of reason's cognitive abilities to determine how in this situation the good might best be attained.[11]

Just as there is no notion of a will in Aristotle, there is also no notion of freedom. This does not at all mean that Aristotle has a view of the world which entails that we are not free. Aristotle's view of the world is such that the behavior of things in the celestial spheres is governed by strict regularity dictated by the nature of the things involved. But once we come to the sublunary, grossly material sphere in which we live, this regularity begins to give out. It turns into a regularity "for the most part," explained by the imperfect realization of natures in gross matter. What is more, these regularities, dictated by the natures of things, even if they were exceptionless, would leave many aspects of the world undetermined. This is not to say that there is anything in the world which, according to Aristotle, does not have an explanation. But the way Aristotle conceives of explanation, the conjunction of these explanations still leaves the world underdetermined in our sense of casual determination. So in Aristotle's world there is plenty of space left for human action which does not collide with, or is excluded by, the existing regularities. Aristotle appeals to this, for instance, when he explains that choosing presupposes that it is up to us, depends on us, whether something gets done or not. Whether it gets done or not is not already settled by some regularity in the world. What is more, Aristotle's universe is not populated by sinister powers who try to thwart us in trying to live the kind of life which is appropriate for beings of our nature. There is a God whose thought determines the natures and thus the regularities in the world as far as they go, and there are truly angelic intellects who move the planets.[12] They should be a source of inspiration for us. They certainly are not a hindrance to our life.

This bright view of the world with plenty of space for free action should not delude us into thinking that we have, according to Aristotle, much of a choice in doing what we are doing. Let us look at Aristotelian choice again. We can choose to do something, if it is up to us to do it or not to do it. This notion of something's being up to us will play a crucial role in all later ancient thought. And it will often be interpreted in such a way that, if something is up to us, we have a choice to do it or not to do it. But, if we go back to Aristotle, this is not quite so. All Aristotle is committed to is that, if something is up to us, we can choose to do it. We can also fail to choose to do it. But to fail to choose to do it, given Aristotle's notion of choice, is not the same as choosing not to do it. We saw this in the case of *akrasia*. One can choose to follow reason. But if one fails to follow reason and acts on a nonrational desire, it is not because one chooses not to follow reason and, rather, chooses to do something else. So the choice one makes in Aristotle is not, at least necessarily, a choice between doing X and not doing X, let alone a choice between doing X and doing Y. It is a matter of choosing to do X or failing to choose to do X, such that X does not get done.

What is more, Aristotle's and, for that matter, Socrates', Plato's, and the Stoics' view of the wise and virtuous person is that such a person cannot fail to act virtuously and wisely, that is to say, fail to do the right thing for the right reasons. But this means for Aristotle that a wise and virtuous person cannot but make the choices he makes. This is exactly what it is to be virtuous. Hence the ability to act otherwise or the ability to choose otherwise, if construed in a narrow or strong sense, is not present in the virtuous person, because it is a sign of immaturity and imperfection to be able to act otherwise, narrowly construed. So long as one can choose and act otherwise, one is not virtuous. So Aristotle's virtuous person could act otherwise only in an attenuated sense, namely, in the sense that the person could act otherwise, if he had not turned himself into a virtuous person by making the appropriate choices at a time when he could have chosen otherwise in a less attenuated sense. Unfortunately, this more robust, less attenuated, sense is not a sense Aristotle is particularly concerned with. And the reason for this is that Aristotle thinks rather optimistically that the ability to make the right choices comes with human nature and a good upbringing. But he also, given the age he lives in and his social background, has no difficulty with the assumption that human nature is highly complex and thus extremely difficult to reproduce adequately in gross matter. Thus he has no difficulty in assuming that most human beings are such imperfect realizations of human nature that they have little or no hope of becoming virtuous and wise. He also has no difficulty with the assumption that most human beings lack a good upbringing. We shall see that this way of thinking will increasingly offend the sensibilities of later antiquity.

Aristotle's view leaves plenty of space for unconstrained human action, but it is hardly hospitable, even in principle, to a notion of a free will. In any case, he lacks this notion. For Aristotle a good life is not a matter of a free will but of hard work and hard thought, always presupposing the proper realization of human nature in the individual, and a good upbringing, which unfortunately many are without.

CHAPTER THREE

The Emergence of a Notion of Will in Stoicism

UNIPARTITE PSYCHOLOGY: REASON, IMPRESSION, IMPULSE, AND ASSENT

As we have seen, for Aristotle to have had a notion of the will, he would have had to have the appropriate notion of a choice. Although he did have a notion of a choice, he did not have the kind of notion which would allow him to say that whenever we do something of our own accord *(hekontes)*, we do so because we choose or decide to act in this way. Aristotle did not have such a notion of choice since he assumed that we sometimes just act on a nonrational desire (i.e., a desire which has its origin in a nonrational part of the soul) without choosing to act in this way and in fact sometimes against our choice. He could assume this, since he supposed that there are nonrational parts of the soul which generate such nonrational desires and that these by themselves suffice to motivate us to act. The crucial assumption is that being hungry may be enough to make you have something to eat and that being angry may be enough to make you take out your anger on the person who made you angry or on someone else.

The underlying conception of the soul as bi- or tripartite, which we find in Plato and in Aristotle, was rejected by the Stoics.[1] Plato and Aristotle had developed their conception of the soul in part in response to Socrates' denial of *akrasia* and his view that, in what we are doing, we are entirely guided by our beliefs. The Stoics took themselves to be reverting to Socrates' view, as they saw it represented in Plato's earlier dialogues, in particular, Plato's *Protagoras*. [2] There is no indication in these dialogues, down to and including the *Phaedo*, of a division of the soul. Even in the *Phaedo* the soul in its entirety seems to be an embodied reason. So the Stoics took the soul to be a reason. They also called it, borrowing a term from Plato's *Protagoras* 352b, *to hēgemonikon*, the governing part of us.[3] It is reason which governs us and our entire life. There is no nonrational part of our soul to generate nonrational desires which would constitute a motivation for us to act quite independent of any beliefs we have and could even overpower reason and make us act against our beliefs. The way we behave is completely determined by our beliefs. If we act utterly irrationally, this is not because we are driven by nonrational desires but because we have utterly unreasonable beliefs. To understand fully why the Stoics reject the partition of the soul, we have to take into account that the opposing view, that the soul has a nonrational part, naturally brings with it two further views: (1) that since it is by nature that the soul is divided, it is also by nature that we have these nonrational desires, and hence it is perfectly natural and acceptable to have such desires, and (2) that these desires, at least if properly conditioned and channeled, aim at the attainment of certain genuine goods, like the food and the drink we need, or at the avoidance of certain genuine evils, like death, mutilation, or illness. This is why we have these desires by nature.

Against this the Stoics argue that these supposedly natural desires, and quite generally all our emotions like anger or fear, are by no means natural. For it is not the case that they naturally aim at the attainment of certain goods and the avoidance of certain evils. According to the Stoics, it is not true that the things the supposedly natural desires and emotions aim to attain or to avoid are genuine goods or evils: the only good is wisdom or virtue, and the only evil is folly or vice. Everything else is indifferent. So it cannot be the case that by nature we have a nonrational part of the soul, so as to be motivated by its appetites and fears to attain certain goods and avoid certain evils. The cause of these appetites and fears is not to be looked for in a supposedly nonrational part of the soul, whose natural emotions they are, but rather in beliefs of reason, namely, in the beliefs that these things are good and hence desirable and that those things are evil and hence repulsive, when, in truth, they are all neither good nor evil but indifferent.

According to the Stoics, the division of the soul threatens the unity of the person and obscures the responsibility we have for our supposedly nonrational desires. It invites the thought that what we are essentially is only the rational part of the soul, which nevertheless cohabits in the body with an unruly, nonrational animal soul and its animal desires. It invites the thought that it is our responsibility to tame this unruly animal, establish the rule of reason in ourselves, and thus create a unified person. It is not our responsibility, but a mere fact of life, that we are confronted and have to deal with this often very strong and beastly animal soul and its crude desires. Against this the Stoics argue that this supposedly nonrational, animal part of our soul with its supposedly nonrational, animal desires is the creation of our mind in the following sense.[4] It is not that we have these desires naturally, because we have a nonrational part of the soul. It is our mind which produces these irrational and often monstrous desires. It is a sheer piece of rationalization to invent a nonrational part of the soul and to devolve on it the responsibility for such desires. They are actually of our own making, because it is our mind or reason which produces them as a result of its beliefs and attitudes.

Aristotle, unlike Plato, had believed that we are not born with reason but with a nonrational soul of the kind other animals have, except that (1) this nonrational soul has an extraordinary capacity to store and process perceptual information and thus to accumulate experience to a degree no other animal can, and that (2) it can not only discriminate recurrent features but also come to recognize them as such. Because of this ability, human beings in the course of their natural development also develop concepts and thus become rational. Reason, as it were, grows out of the nonrational soul with which we are born, to constitute together with this nonrational soul a bi- or tripartite soul.[5] Our upbringing has already involved a conditioning and habituation of this nonrational soul, ideally in such a way as to make it have reasonable desires. Once we have reason, this will greatly affect the way our nonrational soul operates. For now, by having reason ourselves, we can bring it about that the nonrational part of the soul generates only desires which are reasonable. Or we can at least bring it about that when the nonrational part generates desires which are not reasonable, we do not act on these desires. But, however much our nonrational desires may be in line with reason, they in themselves remain the desires of the animal we were born, though now shaped and molded by upbringing and by our own reason. And so long as reason has not acquired perfect control over the nonrational part of the soul, we shall also sometimes continue to act as the animals we were born, namely, to act on mere impulse or on a nonrational desire, instead of a desire of reason.[6]

In contrast, the Stoics believe that in the course of our natural development, we undergo a much more radical metamorphosis.[7] When we are conceived and in our embryonic state, we are plantlike. Our behavior is governed by a nature *(physis)*, as the behavior of plants is. When the embryo is sufficiently developed, the shock of birth transforms this nature into a nonrational soul. We become like animals, acting on the prompting of nonrational desires, on nonrational impulse. But, as we grow up, we develop reason. We come to have concepts and begin to understand how we function and why we behave the way we do. But this reason is not, as in Aristotle and in Plato, a further, additional part of the soul. It is the product of a complete transformation of our innate and nonrational soul into a rational soul, a reason or a mind. This transformation also turns the nonrational desires, with which we grew up and which motivated us as children, into desires of reason. Once we are rational beings, there are no nonrational desires left. They have all become something quite different.

To say that these nonrational desires have become something quite different in becoming desires of reason is to acknowledge that there is some continuity. To see what the continuity is, we have to look briefly at how the Stoics understand the desires or impulses of other animals. They view them very much as Aristotle does. Animals perceive things. This perception involves their having an impression *(phantasia)* of the thing perceived.[8] Now, animals also perceive things as pleasant, satisfying, and conducive to their maintaining themselves in their natural state or as unpleasant, unsatisfying, or detrimental to their maintenance. And so they develop a liking for some things and a dislike of other things. This has an effect on the impressions an animal has. If the animal now perceives something it likes or dislikes, the impression it has takes on a certain coloring. In one case it is an agreeable impression, in the other it is a disagreeable impression. Depending on the complexity of the animal, an agreeable or disagreeable impression may produce memories of past encounters with this sort of thing and expectations about the future. But, whether or not it does so, in the appropriate circumstances the impression in itself, given its coloring, will constitute an impulse either to go after the thing perceived or to avoid it. If a carnivorous animal like a lion feels depleted or hungry, and it has the agreeable impression of a nice piece of meat in reach, this impression in itself will suffice to make it go after the meat. If the little animal to whom the piece of meat belongs in its turn has the disagreeable impression of a lion it is in easy reach of, this disagreeable impression in itself will suffice to impel the little animal to avoid the lion and run away. Such impressions are called "impulsive" *(hormētikai)*, since they impel the animal to act.[9] It is these impressions which constitute the desire of an animal or a child to get something or to avoid something.

According to the Stoics, there is this much continuity between being a child and being a mature human being—that as grown-up human beings we continue to have impulsive impressions. The discontinuity lies in the twofold fact that these impulsive impressions now have a completely different character and that in themselves they no longer constitute an impulse sufficient to impel us to do something. To move us they require an assent of, or acceptance by, reason. It is only if reason accedes to the impulsive impression that it will constitute an actual impulse. So a human impulse, a rational impulse, will have two elements: a certain kind of impulsive impression and an assent of reason to that.

Let us look at these two elements more closely and, to begin with, at the impulsive impressions. According to the Stoics, all human impressions, whether impulsive or not, differ from animal impressions in that they are rational.[10] Animal impressions, being formed in and by a nonrational soul, lack a certain distinctive character which all mature human impressions have, given that they are formed in and by reason: mature human impressions do not just represent something in some way or other but are articulated in such a way as to have a propositional content. They are impressions to the effect that something is the case. Hence they are true or false. Their formation involves the use of concepts, ways of conceiving of things. Thus the Stoics also call such rational impressions "thoughts" *(noēseis)*. Even the perceptual impressions we have when we see something, according to the Stoics, are such thoughts, albeit thoughts produced in a certain way, namely, through the senses.

There is a point here which needs to be emphasized. Clearly, the Stoic idea is that a rational impulse is a compound which has a passive element, namely, the impression, and an active element, the assent. An impression is something you find yourself with. The question is what you do with the impression you find yourself with, for instance, whether you give assent to it. To mark this passive, receptive character of an impression, Zeno, the founder of Stoicism, characterized it as a *typōsis,* an imprint or impression.[11] Hence, Cicero sometimes translates the standard Stoic term for an impression, *phantasia,* by *impressio* (see *Acad.* 2.58). This is how we have come to use the term *impression.*

Already Chrysippus (just two generations after Zeno) objected to this characterization of impressions.[12] I take it that he did so because it is quite misleading in the following respect. It is true that we do not actively form an impression, a certain kind of representation of something, in the way in which we paint a painting or draw a map or describe a person. The impression is formed without our doing anything. But this should not obscure the fact that the way the impression is formed reflects the fact that it is formed in and by a mind. This is why the impressions animals form in their souls will differ from one another depending on the kind of animal in which they are formed, and this is why our impressions differ from the impressions of any other animal in having a propositional content, because they are formed in and by a mind or reason. But, given that, it is also easy to see why the impressions even of the same object will differ among different people, reflecting the difference between different minds. This is bound to be the case, for instance, because not all people have precisely the same concepts or the same habits of thinking about things, the same experiences, or the same beliefs. So it is perfectly true that an impression is something which we find ourselves with. But it is by no means true that we are completely innocent of the particular details of the impressions we individually form. They very much reflect the beliefs, habits, and attitudes of the particular mind in which and by which they are formed.

What is true of impressions in general is also true of impulsive impressions. They are thoughts which reflect your ways and habits of thinking about things. Let us now, though, focus on their impulsive character. Suppose you cut yourself badly with a rusty knife. Given your beliefs, the thought might occur to you that you got infected. And the further thought might occur to you that you might die from this infection. At this point this is a mere impression or thought which you find yourself with. It is a disagreeable, perhaps even disconcerting, thought; that is to say, the mere thought in itself is disconcerting. The question then arises: "What is the source and nature of this disquieting character of the impression?"

According to the Stoics, there are two possibilities. The first is this: you wrongly believe that death is an evil, perhaps even a terrible evil. No wonder, then, that the mere impression that you might die is very disturbing. The second is this: you rightly believe, not that death is an evil but that it is natural to try to avoid death, and that nature means you, other things being equal, to try to avoid death. So the impression that you might die has an alarming character; it puts you on alert. This has a teleological function. It alerts you to the need to be on your guard. And, by a natural mechanism, your whole body will go into a state of alert, ready to move as needed. But the impression, though alarming, is not deeply disturbing. For, after all, you have a clear mind, and you know that there are many false alarms; and even if there is reason for alarm, you as a Stoic know that all you have to do is try to do what you can to avoid death. This is what you are meant to do. You do not actually have to avoid death. That is a matter of divine providence. So the question of whether you are going to die or not in this sense does not affect you at all. This is God's problem, as it were.

But in the case of the person who believes that death is a terrible evil, the alarming character of the impression, which teleologically is just a signal to be on one's guard, turns into a deeply disturbing experience, and as a consequence the whole body goes into a disturbed, perturbed, or excited state, which might affect the operation of reason. Later Stoics will call an impression with such a coloring, and perhaps with the attendant bodily state, a *propatheia,* an incipient passion.[13]

We have to firmly remember, though this might not be so clear to the person in a deeply disturbed state, that so far we are dealing with a mere impression or thought. Naturally, as the thought may occur to you, it may also be false. After all, we have not yet found out, or made up our mind, as to whether we actually got infected. And we have not yet considered whether we should believe that one may die from this infection. So far we have just the mere thought. Now, one cannot be afraid that one might die from this infection unless one believes that one got infected and that one could die from this infection. We clearly have to distinguish between concern and fear, on the one hand, and the alarming or disturbing character of the impression, on the other hand. The wise person will be concerned, but the foolish person who believes that death is an evil will be afraid. Thus fear, according to the Stoics, is nothing but the false belief that an evil is coming, or might come, one's way—a belief generated by assent to an impression which is deeply disturbing because one wrongly takes the situation to be an evil. Sometimes the Stoics also think of fear as the belief coupled with the attendant bodily state.

In the same way in which the Stoics treat a fear, they also treat an appetite, the supposedly natural desire of the non-rational part of the soul. In truth it is nothing but a belief of a certain kind, a belief generated by assent to a highly agreeable impression to the effect that something one conceives of as a good is coming or might come one's way; the highly agreeable and impulsive character of the impression is the result of this mistaken belief that it is a good. The Stoics treat all the emotions, like anger, which are supposed by Plato and Aristotle to originate in a nonrational part of the soul, as misguided beliefs. They call them *pathē*, passions, that is to say, pathological affections, produced by the mind. The Stoic wise man does not experience any such passion. He is *apathēs*. But this does not at all mean that he does not have any emotion. He knows concern, the counterpart of fear; he knows reasonable willing, the counterpart of appetite; and he knows joy, the elated satisfaction at the attainment of a real good, as opposed to gleefulness at the attainment of an imagined good.[14] So much, then, about impulsive impressions and the way they heavily depend on one's own mind and reason.

As to assent, we can now be brief. Animals can do nothing, or at least very little, but rely on their impressions. They have little or no way to discriminate between trustworthy and misleading instances. But *our* impressions are true or false. We also have reason, which allows us to scrutinize our impressions critically before we accept them as true and reliable. Here it is important to remember that there is more to our impressions than their propositional content. This is obvious in the case of perceptual impressions. But we have also seen that a thought that one might die from a certain infection, though it has the same propositional content, might come in different colorings, and the coloring is regarded as part of the thought or impression. So, to give assent to an impression, while primarily a matter of taking its propositional content to be true, is also a matter of accepting it in all its detail, for instance, accepting it, though it is not a clear and distinct impression, and accepting it in its coloring. Given an impulsive impression, one might accept its propositional content but find its impulsive character inappropriate and therefore refuse to assent to the impression on that ground.

There is one last detail which I will merely touch on. The

notion of assent, like its legal counterpart of consent, can be construed quite generously. Just as tacit acquiescence in being ruled or governed by somebody can be construed as assenting to the person's rule, so assenting to an impression does not have to involve an explicit act of acceptance. Not to revolt against an impression but simply acquiescing to it and in fact relying on it can constitute as much an assent as an explicit acceptance.

If we now return to the question of how the Stoics think of the desires Plato and Aristotle characterize as nonrational, it should be clear why the Stoics think that they are all rational, all the product of reason. For the Stoics there is an ambiguity in the term *desire* here. If by *desire* we mean an impulse which actually moves us to action, then, according to the Stoics, we are dealing with a belief of a certain kind that is constituted by reason's assent to an impulsive impression. If, on the other hand, by *desire* we mean, as Plato and Aristotle obviously sometimes do, a motive which might be overridden by a conflicting desire, something which just might move us to act but also may fail to do so, then, according to the Stoics, we must be talking about an impulsive rational impression. And this impulsive impression is formed by reason.

Whatever we make of the details of all this, there is one point which is absolutely crucial for the emergence of the notion of the will. The case of the Stoics against Plato and Aristotle would completely collapse without the assumption that any action, unless one is physically and literally forced into doing something, presupposes an act of reason's assent to an appropriate impulsive impression. This assent will constitute a rational impulse which prompts or drives, as it were, the action. So any human desire *(orexis)* is a desire of reason. Thus any desire of a grown-up human being is a willing, a *boulēsis*. Here, therefore, we do have the notion of a willing which was lacking in Plato and Aristotle, a notion which allows us to say that, when a person does not act by being forced or out of ignorance, the person acts voluntarily or willingly.[15] Among such willings, though, the Stoics now distinguish between *bouléseis* in a narrower sense, namely, reasonable willings, the kind of willings only a wise person has, and appetites *(epithymiai)*, unreasonable willings, which are what we who are not wise have.[16]

So now we have the notion of assent, and hence the appropriate notion of a willing, but we do not yet have the notion of a choice, let alone of a will. To see how we get this, we have to step back a bit. It is clear from what we have said that, according to the Stoics, our whole life is entirely a matter of what we assent to and what not. For our beliefs are a matter of assent, and so are our desires, which are just special forms of belief. Ensuring our life will come out well is entirely a matter of giving assent when that is appropriate and refusing to give assent when it is inappropriate. This focus on our internal life is sharpened by the fact that, according to the Stoics, wisdom is the only good, that a wise life is a good life, and that nothing else matters. So long as one acts wisely, one lives a life of (for us) unimaginable satisfaction and bliss, whatever may happen to one, whether one gets tortured or maimed or killed. The wise person will normally be concerned to avoid such things, but, if they do happen, they will make no difference to him, as he is just concerned to act wisely, by giving assent when appropriate and refusing assent when inappropriate. So the whole focus of one's life now is on one's inner life. And there is a further factor which reinforces this focus, namely, the assumption that the course of the world outside is predetermined. All the wise person can do is try to avoid death, but if he does not manage that, he takes this as a sure sign that nature in her wisdom means him to die and that therefore it is a good thing for him to die. All he has to do, having failed in his attempts to avoid impending death, is to give assent to the thought that it must be a good thing that he is going to die.

Moreover, besides this increasing focus on one's inner life, we also have to take note of the emphasis we find in later Stoics on the assumption that philosophical theory is not an end in itself but a means to living one's life, and their insistence that the application of this theory to one's life requires a great deal of attention to, and reflection on, how one as an individual actually does function, including a great deal of practice *(askēsis)* and exercise in learning to think about things in appropriate ways and to act accordingly. Hence later Stoics will turn to this inner life in a way which is supposed to help us to learn to give assent appropriately. One of these philosophers is Epictetus at the turn from the first to the second century A.D., the most respected and influential Stoic of his time

EPICTETUS AND THE FIRST NOTION OF A WILL

In Epictetus's *Discourses* the notion of *prohairesis* (choice) plays perhaps the central role.[17] It is our *prohairesis* which defines us as a person, as the sort of person we are; it is our *prohairesis* which determines how we behave; it is our *prohairesis* which we need to concern ourselves with more than anything else; indeed, our *prohairesis* is the only thing which in the end matters. Now, given what has been said, we might think that we readily understand this. Since we aim at a good life, our concern should be to give assent to the right impressions and in particular to give assent to the right impulsive impressions, which assent will constitute a rational impulse or desire and make us act in the appropriate way. Therefore we might think that the assent to our impulsive impressions constitutes a choice to act in a certain way and that the *prohairesis* which stands at the center of Epictetus's thought is the disposition of the mind to make the choices which it makes to act in the way we do.

But the matter is more complicated. This is already signaled by the very term *prohairesis.* It should strike us as curious that Epictetus makes such prominent use of a term which is strongly associated with Aristotle and Peripateticism and which had played almost no role in Stoic thought up to this point. We should also remember that in Aristotle willing and choosing are distinguished by the fact that choosing is a matter of willing something which is up to us and in our power.

Clearly, this is highly relevant in Epictetus. In classical Stoicism the phrase "up to us" *(eph' hēmin)* is used in such a way that an action is up to us if its getting done is a matter of our giving assent to the corresponding impulsive impression. Thus it is up to me to cross the street, because whether I cross the street is a matter of my giving assent to the impression that it would be a good thing to cross the street. But Epictetus uses "up to us" in a much narrower way.[18] He insists on taking account of the fact that no external action in the world is entirely under our control. We may not succeed in crossing the street for any number of trivial reasons but ultimately because it may not be part of God's providential plan that we should cross the street. This had been assumed by the Stoics all along, so Epictetus's narrowing of the use of "up to us" hardly constitutes a change in doctrine but rather a shift in emphasis or focus. What Epictetus wants us to focus on is that it is up to us to give, or refuse to give, assent to the impulsive impression to cross the street but that it is not up to us to cross the street. So we can choose to give assent to the impression to cross the street, and we can thus will to cross the street, but we cannot choose or decide to cross the street. It is to make this point that Epictetus resorts to Aristotle's terminology, with its distinction of willing and choosing, and talks of choosing to give assent but of willing to cross the street.

There is another important point which we should take note of. It is conspicuous that assent does not play as central a role in Epictetus as we might expect. He prefers to talk more generally of our "use of impressions" *(chrēsis tōn phantasiōn)* or of the way we deal with our impressions. Assenting to them is just one thing we can do with them, though the most important one. So now it becomes clear, and Epictetus makes this explicit, that what is up to us, what is a matter of our choice, is how we deal with our impressions. We can scrutinize them, reflect on them, try to deflate and dissolve them, dwell on them, and, of course, give assent to them. But giving assent is just one of the things which it is up to us to do, which we can choose to do. And our *prohairesis,* which defines us as the kind of person we are, is not a disposition, as we at first thought, to choose to act in a certain way, because we do not have that choice, but rather a disposition to choose to deal with our impressions in a certain way, most crucially to choose how to assent to impulsive impressions. This assent, which you choose to give, will constitute a willing, and this willing is the impulse which makes you act in a certain way. So this ability and disposition, insofar as it accounts for your willing whatever it is that you will to do, can be called "the will." But the will is called *prohairesis,* rather than *boulēsis,* to mark that it is an ability to make choices, of which willings are just products. This indeed is the first time that we have any notion of a will.

This notion of a will is clearly developed to pinpoint the source of our responsibility for our actions and to identify precisely what it is that makes them our own doings. Chrysippus had said that it is up to us, for instance, to cross the street or not. And he had explained this by saying that it is up to us to give, or refuse to give, our assent to the appropriate impulsive impression. We are now told, according to Epictetus, that the sense of "up to us" involved in the two cases is different. The second case is a narrower and stricter sense of "up to us," whereby it is up to us give or not to give assent to the impression. And we get an explanation of precisely what that means. We can choose or decide to give assent, but we can also choose or decide not to give assent. This choice is to be explained by the will. In explaining your choices, it also explains your willings. But it is not in the same sense up to you to do something or not to do something, since you cannot choose to do something in the way you can choose to give assent.

There are various details here which I will not go into at the length they deserve but which I want to mention at least briefly. The will thus conceived can be a good will or a bad will, depending on whether the choices we make in virtue of it are good choices or bad choices. We may not like the choices we make and therefore not like the will we have. We may will to have a will which makes different choices. We may, for instance, will it to no longer choose to give assent to the tempting impressions we have when we are faced by a delicious piece of cake. So there are second- and higher-order willings which can give the will a great deal of structure and stability. We should also note that the will, as it is conceived here, can choose to give assent to an ordinary nonimpulsive impression, like the impression that it will rain a lot tomorrow, such that, given this assent, we believe that it will rain a lot tomorrow. So in this sense what we believe is a matter of our will, as thus conceived. However, this does not at all mean that we will to believe something. We can at best be said to choose to believe something. For we get a willing only if the will chooses to give assent, not to an ordinary but to an impulsive impression which leads to action. Put differently, not every act of the will is a willing or a volition. Moreover, nothing which has been said so far shows that the will is free in its choices. It can make a particular choice or fail to make a particular choice.[19] But there is nothing in what has been said which forces us to assume, for instance, that it can freely choose whether to give assent or not, or whether to give assent to this impression or another impression. It can choose or decide to give assent to a given impression, but it also can fail to do so.

This notion of the will as our ability to make choices and decisions includes the ability to choose to give assent to impulsive impressions and thus to choose to will to do something. Thus in this complex way it accounts for what other ancient philosophers and we ourselves would call our choosing or deciding to do something. In what follows I shall for the most part focus only on the will as an ability to make choices and decisions as to what to do.

With Stoicism, then, we get for the first time a notion of the will as an ability of the mind or of reason to make choices and decisions. This ability, though, which we all share, in the case of each of us is formed and developed in different ways. How it develops is crucially a matter of the effort and care with which we ourselves develop this ability, which we also might neglect to do. The will thus formed and developed accounts for the different choices and decisions different human beings make. As we have seen, the precise form in which the Stoics conceive of the will depends on their denial of a nonrational part or parts of the soul. Hence in this specific form the notion of a will was unacceptable to Platonists and to Aristotelians, who continued to insist on a nonrational part of the soul.

CHAPTER FOUR

Later Platonist and Peripatetic Contributions

By the second century A.D. Aristotelianism and Platonism had begun to eclipse Stoicism, and by the end of the third century Stoicism no longer had any followers. All philosophers now opted for some form of Platonism, as a rule a Platonism which tried to integrate large amounts of Aristotelian doctrine, including Aristotle's ethical principles. Hence the notion of the will might have easily disappeared from the history of philosophy if Platonists and Peripatetics had not developed their own such notion. This involved retaining the idea that the soul is bi- or tripartite but also taking the crucial step, not envisioned by Plato or Aristotle, that everything we do of our own accord *(hekontes)* presupposes the assent of reason. Now the word *hekōn* has indeed come to mean voluntary or willing.

This change was greatly facilitated by certain remarks in Aristotle and particularly in Plato. We have a tendency, or at least for a very long time have had a tendency, to understand Plato and Aristotle as if they claimed that it were the task of reason to provide us with the right beliefs or, better still, knowledge and understanding, while the task of the nonrational part of the soul is to provide us with the desires to motivate us to act virtuously in light of the knowledge and understanding provided by reason. But we have already seen that this is not the view of Plato and Aristotle. According to them, it is not the task of reason to provide us only with the appropriate knowledge and understanding; it is also its task to provide us with the appropriate desires. To act virtuously is to act from choice, and to act from choice is to act on a desire of reason. The cognitive and the desiderative or conative aspects of reason are so intimately linked that we may wonder whether in fact we should distinguish, as I did earlier, between the belief of reason that it is a good thing to act in a certain way and the desire of reason which this belief gives rise to, or whether, instead, we should not just say that we are motivated by the belief that it is a good thing to act in this way, recognizing this as a special kind of belief which can motivate us, just as the Stoics think that desires are nothing but a special kind of belief.

Further, the modern scholarly view, that according to Plato and Aristotle, reason provides the beliefs and the nonrational part of the soul provides the motivating desires, is grossly inadequate in that it overlooks their view that, just as reason has a desiderative aspect, so the nonrational part of the soul and its desires have a cognitive aspect. This should not be surprising, given that the nonrational part of the soul is supposed to be a close analogue of the kind of soul animals have. Animals have cognition. Indeed, Aristotle is willing to attribute to animals such enormous powers of cognition that some of them, according to him, can display good sense and foresight.[1] Hence we naturally wonder why Aristotle denies reason to animals. The answer is that he, like Plato, has a highly restrictive notion of reason and knowledge, a notion which involves understanding why what one believes one knows is, and cannot but be, the way it is. Reason is the ability in virtue of which we have such knowledge and understanding. It is this kind of understanding which animals are lacking. Obviously, this leaves a lot of conceptual space for less elevated cognitive states which a nonrational soul, and hence an animal, is capable of.[2]

We shall understand this better if we take into account that Plato and Aristotle distinguish three forms of desire, corresponding to the three different parts of the soul, and also, at least sometimes, seem to assume that each of these forms of desire has a natural range of objects which it naturally latches on to. Appetite aims at pleasant things, which give bodily satisfaction; spirit *(thymos)* aims at honorable things; and reason aims at good things. Since both Plato and Aristotle, unlike the Stoics, assume that pleasure and honor are genuine goods, reason can also aim at them, insofar as they are goods. The assumption seems to be that the appetitive part of the soul, though nonrational, can discriminate between the pleasant and the unpleasant. This, presumably, is supposed to serve a purpose. By and large an organism which is not spoiled or corrupted will perceive wholesome food or drink as pleasant, and unhealthy food and drink as unpleasant. So the ability to discriminate between the pleasant and the unpleasant will help the organism to sustain itself, if it is not corrupted in its tastes. When we see a delicious piece of cake, it will be appetite which has the impression that it would be very pleasant to have this piece of cake. Since appetite lacks reason, it has no critical distance from its impression. For it to have this impression amounts to the same as its having this belief. Similarly, the spirited part *(thymos)*, being sensitive to what is honorable, will have the impression that it would be shameful to have yet another piece of cake.

We should also remember that Aristotle explains nonrational desire as originating in the fact that animals not only can perceive things but also perceive them as pleasant or unpleasant. So if you perceive the kind of thing you have experienced as pleasant, without the intervention of reason you have the agreeable impression that there is something pleasant within reach, something which you expect to give you pleasure if you get hold of it. This is an impression and an expectation produced by the nonrational part of the soul. In his remarks on impetuous *akrasia*—cases in which the spirited part of the soul, for instance, in its anger, rashly preempts the deliberation of reason—Aristotle says that those who are prone to this kind of condition do not wait for reason to come to a conclusion but tend to follow their *phantasia*, that is, their impression or disposition to form impressions, rather than their reason (*EN* 7, 1150b19–28). So the akratic sort of person follows an impression formed by or in the spirited part of the soul rather than reason.

Later Peripatetics and Platonists, then, were following Plato and Aristotle in thinking that a nonrational desire consisted of a certain kind of agreeable or disagreeable impression, with its origin in a nonrational part of the soul. They could preserve the division of the soul by supposing that different kinds of impulsive impressions have their origin in different parts of the soul, rather than in reason or the mind, as the Stoics had assumed. But they could now agree with the Stoics (though this in fact meant a significant departure from Plato and Aristotle) that any impression, however tempting it may be, needs an assent of reason to turn it into an impulse that can move us to action. So now reason does appear in two roles. It has or forms its own view as to what would be a good thing to do, and it judges whether to assent or refuse to assent to the impulsive impressions which present themselves. Thus we get the division of reason or the intellect into two parts, as we find in later traditions, for instance, in Thomas Aquinas: a cognitive part and the will.

Another factor which could facilitate this move, as I indicated earlier, is that assent could be construed rather generously as involving simple acceptance of, or acquiescence to, an impression, ceding to it, giving in to it, rather than an active, explicit act of assent. This is why many philosophers were now prepared to say that even nonhuman animals assent to their impressions in that they cede to them and rely on them in their action.[3]

There is an important development in the first century B.C. which further facilitated this change. It is usually claimed that the Stoic Posidonius early in the first century B.C. criticized Chrysippus's doctrine that the passions of the soul have their origin in reason and that he reverted to a tripartite division of the soul. The evidence for this comes from Galen, in particular, Galen's *De Placitis Hippocratis et Platonis,* but it has to be treated with great caution.[4] Galen is an extremely polemical author who shows few scruples in defending or advancing a good cause. He is firmly set against Stoicism and eager to show that on a matter dear to him, such as the division of the soul, the great authority of the school, Chrysippus, who denies this doctrine, has been contradicted by another major Stoic, Posidonius. Hence I have great sympathy with John Cooper's attempt to show that Galen was simply wrong to interpret Posidonius as having thought that there is an irrational part of the soul.[5] On the other hand, it is obvious that Posidonius did criticize Chrysippus and must have said things which allowed Galen to interpret him in this way. What was at issue between Chrysippus and Posidonius?

From the information we have about Chrysippus and the

earlier Stoics, we get the impression that human beings in the course of their natural development would turn into virtuous and wise human beings, if only this development were not interfered with from the outside through corruption from those who raise us and by the society we grow up in.[6] As it is, though, we are made to believe that all sorts of things are good and evil which in fact are neither, and so we develop corresponding irrational desires for or against these things which are entirely inappropriate but which come to guide our life.

I take it that Posidonius questioned this picture. He had an interest in the history of mankind, and he seems to have assumed that there was an idyllic original state of innocence in which people lived peacefully together without coercion, freely following those who were wise.[7] But this original paradisiacal state was lost through corruption, greed, envy, and ambition. Now, this corruption cannot have come from the outside, from society, as society was not yet corrupt. It must have come from the inside, then. If we look for the weak spot on the inside, it must lie in the misguided but tempting impulsive impressions which we find hard to resist. Take, for instance, the case in which one wants to run away because one fears for one's life. For a Stoic this is an unreasonable, inappropriate, and misguided desire, because only evils are to be feared, and death is not an evil. According to the classic Stoic account, the source of this inappropriate desire is the belief that death is an evil. This is not a belief we develop naturally. We acquire it from the outside, because we grow up in a society which believes that death is an evil. Given this belief, the impulsive impression that one might die from an infection takes on a very disturbing coloring and is difficult not to assent to.

Posidonius seems to have asked whether the coloring of the impression must be due to a belief of reason or whether, instead, it could have its origin in a nonrational part of the soul or even in the body and its constitution and state. It could be a natural, nonrational reaction of an organism which sees its life threatened. Similarly, it might be more plausible to refer the coloring of the impulsive impression, not to the mistaken belief that this piece of cake is something good but rather to the body of an organism which is depleted and craving some carbohydrates. It does not matter for our purposes whether Posidonius believed in a nonrational part of the soul. What matters is his suggestion that the impulsive character of at least some of our impressions does not originate in reason's beliefs and thus, ultimately, in some sense, outside us but seems to have its origin in us, for instance, in the particular constitution or state of our body which makes us crave certain things.[8] Peripatetics and Platonists would have gladly taken such considerations as a confirmation of the view that nonrational desires are constituted by impressions which have their origin not in reason but in a nonrational part of the soul.

The second, probably closely connected, development has to do with Stoic analysis of the emotions. If we look, for instance, at Seneca's treatise on anger, we easily get confused, and commentators used to get confused. This is because *anger (ira)* and other terms for emotions, desires, or passions of the soul, are systematically used ambiguously. In classical Stoic doctrine *anger* refers to the desire or impulse one has which makes one act in anger because one has assented to, accepted, and yielded to the relevant impulsive impression. But Seneca also uses *ira* to refer to the mere impression.[9] Later Stoics clarified this ambiguous use of terms like *anger* or *fear* by distinguishing between a *propatheia,* an incipient passion, which is the mere impulsive impression not yet assented to, and a *pathos,* the passion in full force, when the impulsive impression has received assent.[10] This distinction may very well go back to Posidonius. In any case, it would allow Peripatetics and Platonists more easily to identify their nonrational desires with the impulsive impressions they took to be generated by the nonrational part of the soul. They could do this all the more readily since for them, unlike the Stoics, having a desire in itself did not mean that one acted on it.[11] Otherwise they could not have assumed that there could be an acute conflict of desires and that one could act in such a case by following either reason or appetite.

I have so far talked only about what Platonists and Peripatetics would have had to do to get a notion of the will which preserved their assumption of a bi- or tripartite soul and how they could easily have done this, once they accepted the assumption that any action, any doing which we are not made to do by force, presupposes an act of assent. I have not yet done anything to show that this is what Platonists and Peripatetics actually did. Let us begin with assent.

We find this Stoic notion taken over by Platonists in many texts. We know from a fragment of Porphyry's work *On the Powers of the Soul* (ap. Stob., *Ecl.* I.349.19ff) that Longinus doubted whether there was such a thing as the soul's power to give assent. But it seems that Longinus here, as in other respects, was rather singular in his conservatism. I take it that he knew his Plato extremely well and criticized what his fellow Platonists, like Numenius, presented as Plato's philosophy.[12] It was this, I assume, which earned Longinus Plotinus's rebuke that he was a *philologos,* rather than a philosopher (Porphyry, *VP* 14). At a time when Plato was about to become "the divine Plato," Longinus still had no difficulty constantly criticizing Plato's style (see Proclus, in *Tim.* 1.14.7). Longinus was the only significant Platonist of his time who held on to a unitarian rather than a binitarian or trinitarian conception of God. And so we should not be surprised that Longinus, quite rightly, doubted that Plato's philosophy had envisaged a doctrine of assent. But Numenius, the most important Platonist before Plotinus, adopted such a doctrine (see Stobaeus), as did, at least at times, Plotinus and also Porphyry, the student of Longinus and Plotinus (see Porphyry ap. Stob., *Ecl.* II.167.9ff).[13]

We also find this doctrine of assent in the Peripatetics. Thus, for instance, Alexander of Aphrodisias in the *De fato* (XI, p. 178, 17ff Bruns) explains that human beings, unlike animals, do not just follow their impressions but have reason which allows them to scrutinize their impressions in such a way that they will proceed to act only if reason has given assent to an impression. A bit later in the same text (XIV, p. 183, 27ff), Alexander distinguishes between what we do of our own accord *(hekousion)* and what we do because it is up to us *(eph' hēmin)*. Obviously, he has in mind Aristotle's distinction between what we do of our own accord *(hekontes)* and what we do by choice. We remember that the latter class is restricted to actions we will and choose to do, whereas the former also includes those actions which we do when motivated by a nonrational desire (see p. 26). But Alexander now, unlike Aristotle, characterizes this former class as involving a merely unforced assent of reason to an impression, whereas the latter class is supposed to involve an assent of reason based on a critical evaluation of the impression. So it is clear that Alexander takes even an action done on impulse, for instance, an *akratic* action, to involve the assent of reason to the appropriate impression.

Let us return to the Platonists. There are any number of passages which show that Platonists construe following a nonrational desire rather than reason in a similar way. Thus Plotinus

(*Enn.* VI.8.2) raises the question of how we can be said to be free, if it would seem that the impression and desire pull us wherever they lead us. It is clear from the context that Plotinus is speaking about nonrational desires. And it is clear from the curious expression (*hē te phantasia . . . hē te orexis,* with the subsequent verb forms in the singular) that he is identifying the nonrational desire with an impression.

Porphyry (ap. Stob., *Ecl.* II.167.9ff) tells us that somebody whose natural inclinations lead him to act in a certain way could also act otherwise since the impression does not force him to give assent to it. Calcidius, in his commentary on the *Timaeus,* which is taken to reflect a pre-Plotinian source, claims (in section 156) that the soul is self-moved and that its motion consists in assent *(adsensus)* or desire but that this presupposes an impression (or the ability to form impressions) which the Greeks call *phantasia.* Sometimes, though, he continues, this impression is deceptive, corrupts assent, and brings it about that we choose the bad instead of the good. In this case, Calcidius says, we act by being lured by the impression to act in this way, rather than by *voluntas.* So Calcidius, just like Alexander of Aphrodisias (*De fato* XIV, p. 183) and other Platonist and Peripatetic authors, is preserving the distinction between willing *(boulēsis)* to do something, in Plato's and Aristotle's narrow sense, and giving assent in such a way that one can be said to do something willingly in a wider sense, simply because one has assented to it.

It is this wider notion of willing, that is, assenting to an impulsive impression, whether following reason or going against reason, which gives rise to the notion of the will as the ability and disposition to do things by assenting to impressions, whether they have their origin in reason or in the nonrational part of the soul and whether they are reasonable or unreasonable. In this way we come to have a notion of a will in Platonist and Peripatetic authors as, for instance, in Aspasius *(Commentary on Aristotle's Nicomachean Ethics).* [14]

Obviously, this change in the way of looking at nonrational desire has considerable consequences. It is one thing to think of human beings as sometimes being overwhelmed by a powerful desire for something or even to think that reason sometimes is overwhelmed by a powerful desire for something; we readily understand, or believe we understand, how this might happen. It is quite another thing to relocate this conflict as a conflict within reason or the mind. That refocuses our attention on thoughts or impressions. But what is so powerful about these impressions that reason may not be able to resist them?

Classical Stoicism has a relatively easy answer. If impressions have such a power over you, it is because they are formed by reason in a way which reflects your beliefs, and, given these beliefs, it is not surprising if you assent to these impressions. If you think that death is a terrible evil, it is not surprising that you cannot resist the thought to run as fast as you can, if you see death coming your way. It is your reason, your beliefs, which give your impressions their power. But if you do not think that these impressions have their origin in reason and that their power is due to your beliefs, it becomes rather difficult to understand how they would have such a power over reason that, even if they have little or nothing to recommend them rationally, reason can be brought to assent to them. At this point we have to beware of the danger of just covering up the problem by appealing to the free will, by claiming that this is precisely what it is to have a free will—to be able to give assent not only to impressions which with good reason we find acceptable but also to impressions which have no merit rationally. Instead I want to look briefly at some ancient attempts to explain the appealing or tempting character of impressions we wrongly give assent to. Needless to say, we are talking about temptations and about the origins of the very notion of a temptation.

We get a relatively simple and straightforward view in Origen. It is based on the idea that impulsive impressions in themselves have an agreeable or disagreeable character which, in the case of unreasonable impressions, turns them into incipient passions *(propatheiai)*. There may be something titillating about the very impression itself. Origen *(De princ.* III.1.4) speaks of the tickles *(gargalismoi)* and provocations *(erithismoi)* and also the smooth pleasure produced by the impression. Now, you might enjoy the impression and dwell on it. And so it will retain its force or even grow in force. It is perhaps not too far-fetched (though Origen does not say so explicitly) to assume that your ability to form impressions, your imagination, gets encouraged by the way you dwell on the impression, to embellish it and make it seem even more attractive. What Origen does say is that, if you have the appropriate knowledge and practice *(askēsis)*, then, instead of dwelling on the agreeable impression, you will be able to make the impression go away and dissolve the incipient lust. So nonrational and indeed unreasonable impulsive impressions gain some force by our dwelling on and enjoying the agreeable character of the mere fantasy.

When we turn to one of the most influential ascetic writers among the Desert Fathers, Evagrius Ponticus (whose allegiance to Origen stood in the way of his having a greater influence in theology but could not prevent his influence as a spiritual guide), these tempting impressions are referred to as *logismoi* (literally, "reasonings," but here better translated as "thinkings" or "considerations").[15] This is extremely puzzling at first sight, as these impressions have their origin in the nonrational part of the soul or even the body, neither of which can reason. But I have already pointed out that we have to be careful not to overlook the fact that Aristotle, though he denies reason to animals, does not deny animals considerable cognitive abilities and even something which we would call thinking, namely, inferences based on experience. It is just that Aristotle, given his elevated notion of reason as involving understanding, does not call this "thinking." Something similar, mutatis mutandis, can be argued for the Stoics and even for Plato. Correspondingly, while the nonrational part of the soul has no understanding or insight, it is sensitive to experience and can form a view as to how pleasant it would be to obtain something and how, to judge from experience, one might attain it. What it lacks is understanding, especially understanding of the good, which would allow it to understand why it would not be a good thing to indulge in this pleasure.

How can there be *logismoi* which have their origin in the nonrational soul, or even the body, and are able to persuade reason? One way in which this might happen is if reason believes that some pleasures are a good but is not entirely clear about whether *this* pleasure is a good after all. Whereas the nonrational part of the soul is not sensitive to reasons or to reasoning in this sense, reason itself is sensitive to experience and to considerations based on experience. Still, the nonrational part of the soul may learn to become quite persuasive. It might point out how pleasant it would be to obtain a certain object and how easy it would be to obtain it in this circumstance. Reason, as we know, does not require proof, let alone the kind of proof which involves understanding and insight, to be persuaded.[16] So here is the beginning of a view as to how reason might be persuaded to give assent to a nonrational and even unreasonable impression. The nonrational part of the soul offers it considerations, things to be considered in making a choice, which might persuade reason. There is still some puzzle as to how this is supposed to work. We have to explain how reason can be persuaded because it takes these considerations, offered by the nonrational part of the soul, to have some bearing on its own view that it would not be good to indulge in this pleasure. To take the most simple and straightforward case, we need to see why reason, when it thinks that it would not be a good thing to indulge in this pleasure, should in any way be moved by the consideration that it would be very pleasant to indulge in this pleasure. For it to be moved, the nonrational considerations would have to have, or would have to be thought by reason to have, some bearing on its own view.

But now it looks as if reason, to give assent to the nonrational impression, would have to change its own view, in the sense that it rationalizes into a rational impression the nonrational impression that it would be pleasant to indulge in this pleasure—an impression of reason that it would be good to indulge and so give assent to this rational impression and thus, indirectly, to the nonrational impression.[17]

We do find a view like this in Plotinus (*Enn.* VI.8.2). The question here is in what sense we are free to do what we want to do and are not just driven and made to do what we do by the things around us. If these things produce impressions and nonrational desires in us, and these desires make us act the way we do, these actions are not our actions in any substantial sense but things we are made to do, things which just happen to us. If we say that our actions are not simply the product of desire but also of the considerations of reason *(logismoi)*, we have to ask whether the considerations of reason produce the desire or whether the desire produces the considerations of reason. If the latter, our action again will not be ours in the substantial sense we are looking for, because, though it involves rational considerations on our part, these are just rationalizations of our nonrational desire, which in turn is produced by the object of desire.

This way of looking at things produces yet another notion of the will: the impressions the will assents to, or refuses to endorse, as in Stoicism, are all impressions of reason. But there is a crucial distinction between these impressions. Some are just the reflection of our grasp on, or our understanding of, our insight into reality, whereas others are the result of our rationalization of our nonrational desires. Plotinus calls the state of the soul in which we have such pure rational impressions "intellectualization" (VI.8).[18] We shall return to Plotinus later in detail. What is of interest here is that Plotinus's view would make it intelligible how reason would not simply fall silent and cave in to a nonrational desire but would, as the notion of a will requires, actively endorse it by assenting to an impression which is due to rationalization of the desire or the corresponding impulsive impression.

The world of later antiquity is populated not only by all the things we can see and touch but also by myriads of transparent and intangible beings or even incorporeal beings—in short, daemons of various kinds. They are not necessarily rational beings, but especially if they are, they might take an interest in us, as we might take an interest in them. For, given their mobility or their form of presence or just their sheer power of mind, they do, or easily can, know lots of things hidden from us. They can also be extremely powerful; given their knowledge of how the physical world works, they can manipulate nature. Some of them are good and benevolent; these are angels. Others are downright evil and malevolent. These daemonic beings may or may not have any direct power over our intellect, as our intellect *(nous)* is not part of nature or at least not subject to natural necessity. But, thanks to their knowledge of how nature works, they do have power over our bodies. And since in late antiquity one more and more comes to think that the state of the nonrational part of our souls not only to some extent depends on one's bodily state but is even more or less a function of it, these daemons also have considerable power over the nonrational part of the soul. They can induce in you nonrational impressions and desires. These are the temptations of the devil. If your reason works in such a way that it follows these desires, for instance, by rationalizing them, they can also in this way manipulate your reason. And they are extremely good at this, because your mind or your soul is an open book to them.

Augustine (*Contra Academicos* I.17) tells us the following story. There was in his student days in Carthage a man called Albicerius, who possessed an uncanny knowledge which one should not confuse with wisdom. One could go and consult this man about where one had misplaced one's silver spoon or what happened to money which had disappeared. Albicerius always knew the answer, though he had little education. One day Flaccianus, who did not believe in such superstition, went to test Albicerius. He asked Albicerius what he, Flaccianus, had been doing in the morning. Stunned by getting the correct answer in full detail, he went on to ask Albicerius what he, Flaccianus, was thinking right now. Albicerius could tell him not only "a verse of Vergil" but also which verse, uneducated though he was.

Now one might think that Augustine, and his young friends too, especially after their conversion, would not believe any of this. But, to the contrary, they, like most of their contemporaries, had no difficulty in believing that Albicerius was availing himself of daemons who had access to one's thoughts. It is no wonder that in a world like this, in which even a little insignificant daemon might have such powers, people might wonder whether our choices and decisions were free. And this all the more so, as there was also the widespread belief that we, in turn, if only we knew how, might make daemons or even gods do what we want them to do, rather than what they would want to do, if they had not been coerced. So we will next turn to the question of how the notions of freedom and a free will emerged.

CHAPTER FIVE

The Emergence of a Notion of a Free Will in Stoicism

Stoic views, as we have already noticed, often seem rather counterintuitive in the sense that they fly in the face of what we commonly believe to be true and take for granted. The Stoics, of course, are perfectly aware of this. They take all of us (and they do not exclude themselves) to be corrupted in our beliefs and attitudes, to be foolish. This is why we find some of their views counterintuitive. By formulating pithy sayings, which came to be known as the *Paradoxa Stoicorum,* the Stoics go out of their way to shake us out of the complacency with which we take our beliefs for granted, however foolish they may be. One such paradox is this: Only the wise person is free, everybody else is a slave. Obviously, they do not mean that we are all slaves in the legal or political sense or that only the wise person is politically free, just as they do not mean that only the wise person is a king in the political sense, when they say that only the wise person is a ruler. So what do they mean, when they say that only the wise man is free?

There is a Stoic definition of freedom *(eleutheria)* which may go back to Chrysippus and came to be fairly widespread (DL 7.121 [LS 67M]). According to this definition, freedom is a matter of having the ability to act on one's own, to act at one's own discretion, to act on one's own account, to act independently. The Greek is *exousia autopragias.* It is not immediately clear from the mere language precisely what is meant, especially since the word *autopragia,* like its cognates, *autoprageō* and *autopraktos,* is extremely rare. It almost always occurs in the context of this definition and apparently is a Stoic coinage. Perhaps we can get a better sense of what it might mean, at least provisionally, if we look at what it might mean to say that people who are not wise are not free but slaves. Here it is relatively clear what is intended. According to the Stoics, the mark of the foolish person is that he takes a lot of things to be goods and evils which in truth are neither, for instance, life, health, strength, good looks, a good reputation, power, wealth, and their opposites. As a result the foolish person develops an inappropriate attachment to, or revulsion from, these things which he takes to be goods or evils. This attachment or revulsion constitutes an enslavement, because it prevents the foolish person from doing what he would reasonably want to do in pursuit of his own good. It is these presumed goods and evils which become his masters, run and determine his life, in that they now make him compulsively go after them or run away from them, without regard for what he would need to do if he were to follow his own true interest. It is the objects of the person's fears and appetites, and the unrealistic fantasies they give rise to, which determine the person's actions and life, rather than the person himself.

Aristotle had insisted that one is not responsible for what one does, if one is literally forced to do it or made to do it. And this made good sense, since something which we are just made to do is not our own action, since it is not in any way motivated by a desire on our part. This meant construing *force* quite narrowly, so that the paradigm would be sheer physical force, physical compulsion. But Aristotle was willing to extend this notion of being forced to cases of psychological compulsion to the extent that a psychological force which no human being could possibly resist counts as exculpating.[1] For, if one acts under such force, this still does not reveal anything about the particular sort of person one is, about one's motivation. What we now get with Stoicism, and in the wake of Stoicism, is an enormous expansion of what counts as being forced *(biazesthai)*, or compelled, or made to do something, and correspondingly an enormous contraction of what counts as an action of one's own, properly speaking, as an action the initiative for which lies in oneself, rather than on the outside in the presumed goods or evils. This shift, at least in the case of the Stoics, does not, however, involve a corresponding shift of the boundary between the responsible and the nonresponsible, especially since the person himself by his own doing has enslaved himself in this way so as to act henceforth under compulsion. So the idea would be this: freedom is the ability to act on one's own initiative, as opposed to being compelled to act the way one does, running after some things and avoiding others, because one has enslaved oneself to them.

Not just the term *autopragia* needs some attention but also the word *exousia*. It too is not a particularly common word, and, given its uses, it might well mean something a lot stronger than the bland ability I have spoken of so far, such as one's freedom of action as authorized by law or the authority of one's office. This latter is clearly what it does mean in a passage in Origen *(Comm. in Ioan.* I.4; II.16).[2] Origen tells us that the Stoics claim that only the wise are free, since they have attained the *exousia autopragias* by divine law. And he adds that they define *exousia* as lawfully delegated power. So there is divine law, namely, the order which God has imposed on things, the order according to which things happen in the world. It is part of this order that, if you do not sell yourself into slavery, then you are allowed to act on your own initiative. If you do enslave yourself, you are no longer able, given the way God has arranged things, to do so. You are no longer a free citizen in God's world, as it were.

There is a problem here. The wise man is free, because he has liberated himself from his false beliefs and inappropriate attachments. But what are we to say about those who are not yet wise but also have not yet enslaved themselves? Epictetus (1.19.9) considers the case of somebody who is threatened by a tyrant with the worst threats. If he values his will *(prohairesis)*, Epictetus retorts, he will say to the tyrant, "God made me free."

To understand this, we have to go back to the very beginning, to God's creation of the world. God, given his wisdom and goodness, could not but create the best possible world. But there are various ways to understand what it is for a world to be the best possible. One way is to assume that there are, independent of the creator or demiurge, a certain number of goods and a certain number of evils, and that a world is the best possible if it has a minimum of these evils and a maximum of these goods. This, I take it, is not a promising line to take if the creator is God himself, at least if we take God to be a first principle or even the first principle, that is, something in terms of which everything else is to be explained but which itself does not require any explanation. For, if the creator is God, there will be no answer to the question of where the goods and evils which the creator tries to maximize and minimize, respectively, come from and how they acquire their status as goods and evils. They now look as if they were something antecedent to God by which God is bound in his creation. This, though, would violate not only the idea that God is a first principle but also the idea that God is not bound by any external, antecedent constraints in what he is doing. Here, then, is another approach.

The creator is called a demiurge, that is to say, we are invited to look at the world as a piece of craftsmanship, like a house or a car. Now we have some idea of what it would mean to build a very good house or a very good car. We can look at a house, at its various details, to see how well the builder has built it, within the limitations and specifications which the person who ordered the house set down in advance. Whichever detail we look at, we try to see whether the builder could have done better. But however hard we think, and however knowledgeable we may be about house building, we may find nothing to criticize. It seems to me that it might be possible to distinguish two senses in which a house or a car might be a good house or a good car. Suppose that, after checking the building, you find that the builder built you a house exactly according to your specifications. It is all very solidly and reliably done. You are perfectly content with what the builder did. He obviously knows his craft. You think it is a good house. But in checking the house you might discover that it was a good house in not just this first sense; you might also come to marvel at the ingenuity, resourcefulness, thoughtfulness, and creativity with which all this has been done. The difference between the first and second assessments is not necessarily that, on the second one, the house comes out to be less expensive, more functional, or better serving the needs for which you wanted the building. This may be true, too. But it is not crucial for my point. What is crucial, rather, is that, especially if you know something about building, you might come to think that the house is a genuinely wonderful building which in all details, as you look at them, constantly surprises you and makes you marvel at the mastery of the art which has gone into it. It is a real joy to look at.

The point perhaps becomes clearer if we look at the matter from the builder's point of view. In the first case, we have a builder who sets out to build you a house, according to the rules of the art, which will fit your specifications. This is his job. But look at the second builder in this way: for him building your house is just an occasion, a pretext, as it were, to exercise his mastery of the art. Of course, he can build you a good house in the first sense. This is not the slightest problem for him, and he can be absolutely relied on to do so. But for this very reason, that also holds little interest for him. What he is really interested in does not lie in building a good house in the first sense. He has set his ambition higher. He wants to do what he can do well anyway but with the utmost ingenuity; he wants to exercise his superb mastery of the art. He actually enjoys his mastery of the craft. With this, it seems to me, we have arrived at a much more elevated sense of a good house.

We can now go back to the world. We are now supposed to believe that, if we scrutinize the details of the world, however much we think about it in light of what we know about how one could organize a world, we will find nothing to criticize. To the contrary, the longer we look at it, and the better we understand it, we cannot but be overawed by the resourcefulness and creativity of the mind that created it. In fact, we come to believe that it would not be possible to create a world better than this. We come to be so taken with this marvelous arrangement and order of things that we wish we could do something like this but also recognize what our limited place in this order is.

Before we proceed with this doxology, let us take note of a corollary. Obviously, this world would not be much good if the living beings in it did not have a sufficient supply of food to keep them going, if they got so easily damaged that they could not function properly for the most part, or if, at the slightest occasion, they dropped dead. It would be a world which would be difficult to maintain. One would constantly have to re-create whole species. We easily see now why nature privileges supply of food over lack of food, health over illness, life over death, physical integrity over mutilation, and so on. This does not mean, though, that these things are goods or evils. Their status is just a result of the kind of world God created. Given this kind of world with living beings in it, it would not be a good world if life and health and the rest were not, other things being equal, systematically favored over their opposites. Indeed, the Stoics call them "preferred" things *(proēgmena)* and their opposites "dispreferred" *(aproēgmena)*.[3] But to be a preferred thing is not to be a good thing. After all, these preferred things can be misused and will be of advantage to their owner only if used wisely. So one would be perfectly right to believe that it is a good thing to look after one's health. But there are two ways to believe this. One is to believe, as Plato generally and Aristotle always does, that health is a good and therefore it is a good thing to look after one's health. The other way is to believe that health is a preferred thing and hence to believe that looking after one's health (as distinct from health as such) is a good thing, since it contributes to the way the world is supposed to be.[4] There will be a corresponding difference in the desire of reason, which the belief that it is a good thing to look after one's health constitutes or gives rise to. In the first case, it will be an irrational appetite; in the second case, it will be a reasonable willing.

Now, if we look at how God arranged the world, we see that he has created living things in such a way that they largely manage to take care of themselves; they are self-maintaining systems. God does not have to maintain them; he has arranged things in such a way that they maintain themselves. As the complexity of the organism increases, this system of self-maintenance also becomes increasingly complex and sophisticated. Thus, when we come to animals, they are constructed in such a way as to monitor their own state and have an awareness of what they need to get and what they need to avoid to maintain themselves. Hence, when they encounter an object of a relevant kind in their environment, this will produce an agreeable or disagreeable impression in the animal, and this impression in turn will cause the animal to move either towards the object or away from it.[5] So the animal is constructed in such a way that it, by and large, is made to do what it needs to do by the objects which are conducive or detrimental to its maintenance.

In the case of human beings, though, the arrangement is even more ingenious. God constructs them in such a way that they can recognize for themselves what they need to do to maintain themselves (as long as they themselves are needed) and hence will maintain themselves of their own choice and understanding. He constructs them in such a way that they develop reason, and with reason an understanding of the good, and thus come to be motivated to do of their own accord what needs to be done.[6] So, instead of constructing them in such a way that they are made to do what they need to do to maintain themselves, he constructs them in such a way that they do this of their own initiative and indeed can do it wisely, showing precisely the kind of wisdom, ingenuity, resourcefulness, and creativity on a small scale, namely, the scale of their life, which God displays on a large scale. In this way, if they are wise, human beings genuinely contribute to the optimal order of the world, and they find their fulfillment in this. This is what the good life for the Stoics amounts to.

If we now look back at freedom as the *exousia autopragias*, it should be clear that what *autopragia* here refers to is our ability, unlike other animals', to do the things that need to be done, solely guided and motivated by our own understanding of things, rather than just being made to do things. And *exousia* indicates that this is a special gift or privilege. For it answers our natural wish, once we come to have some understanding of the world, that it would be wonderful to be able to arrange things as wisely and ingeniously as God does. This wish has been granted in a modest way. We have been given the ability to arrange things within the context of our life wisely and ingeniously, resourcefully and creatively. God has left it to our discretion how we wisely and ingeniously maintain ourselves. But there is the divine law Origen referred to. It is part of the order of things that we have this ability, that we have this freedom, only so long as we proceed wisely, in the way a wise person would do, in maintaining ourselves. It will be wise, if we need some food, to get the food we need. But it will not be wise to have twice or thrice the amount of food we need, to become addicted to food, to enslave oneself to food. For then it will be the food which makes one eat compulsively. One will have lost one's ability of *autopragia*.

There is another term which seems to be of Stoic origin and refers to this ability to act of one's own initiative, namely, *to autexousion*. The term is twice found in the fragments of Musonius and then more often in Epictetus. It comes to be used by Platonists and Peripatetics but also from Justin Martyr onwards very frequently by Christian authors.[7] Not surprisingly, the term is often translated as if it meant "having a free will." But, strictly speaking, it just refers to the ability of a person to do what needs to be done of his own initiative, rather than being made to do it or ordered to do it; it refers to the freedom of the person to act as he sees fit in pursuit of the good.

Now, we also have to remember that, according to the Stoics, we are not born as rational beings, that we are not born with reason.[8] Hence we are also not free when we are born but function like animals, being made to do things. So, when it is said that we are created free, this must mean that we are created in such a way that we would naturally develop into free agents, as we develop reason. So in this sense all human beings are created free. But it also turns out, at least in standard Stoic doctrine, that, as we develop reason under the influence of society, we immediately espouse false beliefs about the value of things and thus enslave ourselves.[9] So we never actually are free before enslaving ourselves. For freedom requires reason, and, as we are acquiring reason, already in the process of acquiring it we are enslaving ourselves. This is why only the wise man in fact is free.

One further point needs at least to be mentioned, though it deserves more detailed consideration. It is clear from the Stoic claim that only the wise are free, that freedom, like wisdom and virtue, does not admit of degrees.[10] If you admit just one inappropriate attachment, you have lost your freedom. Ultimately, the reason for this is that the Stoics think all your beliefs, desires, and attitudes form one system and that the influence which the elements in this system have on you is in part due to the position they have in this system, which is defined by the logical relations between the constituent elements. Thus, if you add a false belief to your system, it undermines all the true beliefs you have which are incompatible with the false belief. And if you add one inappropriate attachment, it undermines all the appropriate attachments incompatible with it. It affects your entire motivational system and thus the force of its constituent elements. So even your best motivational system in a particular case will be tainted by your inappropriate attachment, however large the logical distance, as it were, between the two may be. Your will, in order to be free, has to be absolutely pure.

With this we can turn to the freedom of the will. For we now have a notion of a will and a notion of freedom, and we need to see how and why the two notions come to be combined in the notion of a free will.

We have noted how Epictetus admonishes us to concentrate all our efforts on our will, on the way we make choices and decisions. The goodness or quality of people is a matter of the goodness or quality of their will (1.29.1). To be good the will has to be such that it accords with nature, that is to say, it has to be such as it is intended to be by nature or God. But by nature, we are told, the will is intended to be free (1.4.18). Epictetus claims that he wishes it to be his main concern, up to the very last moment of his life, that his will be free (3.5.7). What is it for the will to be free?

Epictetus explains again and again that this is a matter of the will's not being prevented from making the choices it sees fit to make, of its being impossible to force it to make any choice other than it would want to make (1.12.9; 1.4.18; 3.5.7). There is no force or power in the world which can force your will so long as it is free. The planets cannot force your choice. Even God cannot take away your free will and force your choice (1.1.23). Nor, Epictetus explains (3.3.8–10), would God want to do so. For, after all, he has given you a will of the kind he himself has, a will which, so long as it is free, cannot be forced or hindered in making choices. The situation completely changes once we attach our hearts to things in the world, make ourselves dependent on them, become addicted to them, enslave ourselves to them. Then the world begins to have an enormous power over us, and we begin to act under compulsion. We become dependent on, or the victims of, the course the outside world takes in presenting us with sup- posed goods and evils.

So here we have our first actual notion of a free will. It is a notion of a will such that there is no power or force in the world which could prevent it from making the choices one needs to make to live a good life or force it to make choices which would prevent us from living a good life. But it is a notion such that not all human beings in fact have a free will. They are all meant by nature to have a free will, that is, each human being is capable of having a free will. But human beings become compulsive about things and thus lose their freedom. Hence only the wise person has a free will.[11]

To get clearer about this particular notion of a free will, if we remember our general schema for a notion of a free will (see chapter 1, p. 7), we have to clarify one further detail. We are free to make the choices we need to make to live a good life, unless we enslave ourselves, because the world is not such that there are any forces or powers which can force our choices, so long as we retain the freedom of the will. But, we have to ask, does not God constrain what we can do and at least in this indirect way, if not directly, constrain what we can choose? How can we be free to choose what we could reasonably want to choose or even what we would need to choose to have a good life, if God has predetermined all along what is going to happen and hence also what we are going to do? How can the will be free, if all our actions are predetermined? Only if we pursue this question in some detail will we get at some further massive assumptions which underlie this first notion of the free will.

The Stoics assume that everybody is either wise and free or foolish and enslaved. The case of the foolish person, because his will is not free, as he has enslaved himself, is not a problem. Still, it is worth our while briefly to consider it. The person who is foolish will do foolish things or will do the right things but for foolish reasons. What we have to focus on here is what the fool actually does in the world, what happens in the world. We have to set aside, as a different problem, how it can be part of the best possible world that foolish things get done, for instance, that somebody kills somebody for no good reason and that there are foolish people. But, given that the foolish person does not have a free will, he poses no problem for God's arranging the world as he sees fit, so far as what happens in the world is concerned. Whether it is part of the divine plan that the foolish person does something foolish or whether it is part of the plan that the person does something which is not foolish, God has ways to bring this about, given that the person does not have a free will. God just has to set up the circumstances in such a way that the person will be forced to do what he is meant to do. If it does not fit the divine plan that the foolish person does something, whether it is foolish or not foolish, God has only to set up the circumstances in such a way that either the foolish person in these circumstances has no motivation to do what he is not meant to do or, though he is motivated to do what he is not meant to do, circumstances interfere with his carrying out what he is motivated to do and hence tries to do. The foolish person goes out to do something, but he is run over (let us say) by a car.

Now, if we turn to the wise person, the situation is radically different, since his will is free. In his case, to ensure that the world proceeds according to the divine plan so that it will be the best possible world, God cannot simply set up the circumstances in such a way that the person will be forced to act in the desired way. But God does not have to do anything to bring about the wise and free person's compliance. For it is part of the wisdom of that person to know the good thing to do in a given circumstance and to be motivated to do it, given his attachment to the good. And since the good thing to do in a given circumstance is what nature means one to do or what God wills one to do, the wise person will do what, according to the divine plan, he is meant to do, namely, the best possible thing to do in this situation. So God will do nothing to thwart the wise person's action or prevent it from being carried out.

Actions like this are the only free actions which ever occur out there in the world, as opposed to things which happen in our minds. But we need to look more closely at how they are explained. They are motivated by an understanding and an attachment to the good, meaning the wise order of the world, and the recognition in a particular situation that, to contribute to and to maintain this order, a certain course of action will be the most appropriate. Such understanding and recognition, at least in this pure form, would not be possible if the will were not free. For one's attachment to things other than the good would blur one's recognition of the best thing to do in a given circumstance. So the wise person is solely motivated by his correct understanding of the good and his attraction to it. What he chooses or decides to do, because it is the best thing to do, is what God wills him to do. However, his action is not motivated by what God wills but by his recognition and understanding that this is the best thing to happen in these circumstances. And, because God himself also sees that this is the best thing to happen in these circumstances, God wills it to happen. So the wise person's will and the divine will coincide. But it is not the case that what motivates a free action is that God wills it.

Things are complicated, however, by the fact that human wisdom is limited. Even the wise person is not omniscient. Even the wise person, though he will have a good understanding of the natural order of things, through no fault of his own is often in a concrete situation where he will not know the best thing to happen and why this would be so. Even the wise person is often limited to conjecture. Thus he might still look after his health, when, according to the divine plan, he is already about to die. But the wise person will recognize from the futility of his best efforts to restore his failing health that he is about to die. He still might not understand why it would be the best thing for him to die soon. In this case, he will assume that it must be the will of God that he die soon, and he will act accordingly. He will want to die, because he recognizes that this is what God wills. But again it is not the sheer recognition of God's will which makes him will to die. It is, rather, his counting on the fact that there are good reasons why God wills him to die, albeit reasons which he himself cannot clearly identify. It is against this background that we have to understand Epictetus's repeated remarks that our willing should accord with God's will, that we should will what God wills.[12]

But let us return to free action. This is accounted for in terms of a free choice of the will. Does this mean that the free choice of the will does not have any explanation? Not at all. The free agent freely gives assent, freely chooses to give assent to the impression that it would be a good thing to act in this way in this situation. And there is an explanation for this choice. It lies in the fact that the agent understands why it would be a good thing to act in this way in this situation and he is utterly attached to the good. Is there an explanation for this understanding and this attachment? Yes, there is an explanation in terms of antecedent causes of how the agent came to have this understanding and attachment. It is a story which goes back to the birth of the person and beyond, as far as we care to trace it. But how, in this case, can the choice of the person be said to be free?

At this point we again have to step back a little bit. Already, according to Chrysippus, who did not yet have a notion of free will, we are responsible for what we do if our action has its origin in the fact that we give assent to the appropriate impression.[13] The fact that we give assent, rather than refuse to give assent, reflects on us in such a way that we are responsible for what we did. Chrysippus insists that we cannot say that the impression of an object, however tempting it may be, necessitates our assent to it, and hence our choice. For human nature is not such that any human being, just because he is a human being, will give assent to the impression. It is not a law of human nature, as it were, to give assent to this sort of impression. We know this because other human beings may not give assent to such an impression. So, if you give assent, it must be because you are the person you are. Hence it is up to you to give assent or not in the sense that it depends on you, on the kind of person you are, whether you give assent. And the claim that the impression does not necessitate your assent is backed up by a bit of Chrysippean modal logic. Chrysippus defines possibility in such a way that a statement of the form "It is possible that A is F" is true, precisely if the nature of A does not exclude its being F, and if the circumstances in which A finds itself do not prevent A from being F.[14] Hence, if in certain circumstances you give assent to this impression, it is also possible for you not to give assent to this impression. For human nature does not exclude your not giving assent to the impression, as we can see because other human beings do not assent to this sort of impression. Nor are the circumstances such as to prevent a human being from not giving assent to this impression. So, in any case, the assent the person gives to an impression is not necessitated, given that, on this notion of possibility, it is possible for the person not to give assent and hence not to act in this way.

But, having moved beyond Chrysippus, we now also, in addition to the notion of necessitation, have the notion of being forced. Given this notion, we shall say that the assent of the person whose will is not free, though it is not necessitated, is nevertheless forced. A person who does not have a free will is forced to assent; if the appropriate object of desire shows up, it provokes the appropriate kind of impression which will make the agent assent to it. Here is a causal sequence with a lawlike regularity. But the case of the free person is entirely different. Any object may show up; it may produce an impression in him, but this impression is not going to force him to give assent. For we have already seen that what makes him give assent is not the impression but his understanding that it would be best to pursue or to avoid the object, and his attachment to the good. But, if this is what makes him give assent, why should we not say that it forces him to give assent, so that the free person's assent is as much forced as the unfree person's?

To do so would be highly misleading. To begin with, the unfree person's assent is forced by the impression, whereas the free person's assent, if at all forced, is not forced by the impression. It is brought about, rather, by the free person's understanding and insight. The free person could not, given this understanding and insight, choose otherwise, except by sacrificing his rationality, which he is not prepared to do. Somebody who is perfectly rational will simply choose this way. We can, of course, say that somebody who accepts certain premises and sees that a certain conclusion follows from them is forced to accept the conclusion on pain of giving up his rationality. But this sense of *forced* is entirely different from the sense in which the unfree person's assent is forced. What is more, this sense of *forced* does not stand in the way of saying that a person who is free has a will which is free to choose what one would reasonably choose, that is to say, is in no way hindered, hampered, or prevented from making the choices which one would reasonably want to make. His understanding and his insight might make the free person choose what he does, but they certainly do not prevent him or hinder him from making the reasonable choice or force him to make a choice which is not reasonable.

We can explain the free person's understanding and insight in a similar way, in terms of antecedent causes, for instance, of his coming to have certain true beliefs. These true beliefs were not forced on this person, nor did his having these true beliefs force this understanding on him. Indeed, there is a long story, beginning with the person's birth, which explains how he came to have these true beliefs and how he came to have this understanding. It is, in the ancient understanding, a causal story. But it does not involve reference to any force which would make us question whether the choice of the free person was free, given that it had this chain of antecedent causes.

But before we turn to this story, we have to take into account another fact. By the time we come to Epictetus, it is thought that there are three crucial factors involved in one's birth, namely, human nature, one's individual nature and constitution, and the circumstances into which one is born.[15] Now, if the Stoics want to assume that all human beings are free by nature, they must also assume that none of these factors is such that it, separately or in conjunction with the others, will prevent us from developing in such a way as to have the insight and the understanding it takes to make the right choices. This is a substantial assumption about God's creation. God must set things up in such a way that neither human nature nor our individual nature nor the circumstances into which we are born, either separately or jointly, prevent us from becoming wise and free. Indeed, the Stoics not only assume this, they also assume that God sets things up in such a way that we all, in the course of our natural development, could acquire the understanding and the insight to make the right choices. God constructs human beings in such a way that they could naturally acquire true beliefs.

It is not that God constructs human beings so as to have beliefs, and it just so turns out that some of them are false and some of them are true. Rather, God constructs human beings in such a way that we are highly sensitive to truth and predisposed to form beliefs that are naturally true. Hence our having the true beliefs we have does not require an explanation, though we can specify the mechanisms by means of which we come to have them. What does require explanation is our having false beliefs. They must be due to the fact that something went wrong, interfering with the natural process which would have led to our having just true beliefs. And the Stoics identify what went wrong with our giving assent to a false impression, when we should give assent only to those true impressions which are recognizably true. Moreover, we are constructed in such a way that, once we have the appropriate true beliefs, we will also naturally come to have sufficient understanding of the world and thereby a sufficient understanding of the good, so as to be attracted by it and make the right choices. Again, what needs an explanation is not how we get there, though one can specify the mechanisms involved. What needs an explanation is why we do not get there, because something has gone wrong. And the answer again is that we ourselves abort this natural development by being rash, careless, or impatient in the way we give assent.

Here, then, we have, for the first time in history, a notion of a free will, a will which is not forced in its choices and decisions and hence is free to make the right choices. It is not an ability to make choices which no sane person would want to make. But we should note that it is deeply embedded in a theory which makes massive assumptions about the world, about ourselves, and about our position in the world. The assumptions about ourselves are mainly embodied in the notion of the will. But there is in addition the assumption that the world down to the smallest detail is governed by a good and provident God and that this God, in creating the world, has made sure that neither human nature nor our individual nature and constitution nor the circumstances into which we are born, nor the conjunction of these three factors, would prevent us from developing in such a way as to be able to make the right choices and decisions in our life. He has also arranged things in such a way that, unless we are going to enslave ourselves, no force or power in the world can force our will not to make the right choices, not even God himself. These are massive and powerful assumptions which one would do well at least to question and which certainly were not shared by everybody in antiquity. This can in no way be an ordinary notion which everybody had had all along.

How substantial it is we can see from the fact that, considered in hindsight, Aristotle's view is incompatible with the assumption that human beings by nature have a free will or at least this notion of a free will. For, in Aristotle's view, many human beings are barred by their natural constitution and the circumstances into which they are born from ever having a free will. We also immediately see why this was acceptable for Aristotle, and to a lesser extent for later Peripatetics, but would not be acceptable for Stoics. Unlike the Stoics, Aristotle did not believe in a benevolent God whose providence reaches down to the smallest details. For the Stoics the thought that human beings by birth might be excluded from freedom, wisdom, and a good life was intolerable. But for Aristotle this was perfectly acceptable. After all, Aristotle was even willing to justify the social institution of slavery on the ground that many human beings by nature are slaves.[16] While he insists on the goodness of the world and the claim that God is the source of this goodness,[17] Aristotle also seems to think that the good order of the world naturally starts to give out at the point where the details are too trivial to affect its goodness overall.

Once we have isolated the assumptions and concerns which give rise to this first notion of a free will and the questions it was meant to help us answer, we have to ask whether these are the assumptions, concerns, and questions we ourselves have and hence whether we have any need for such a notion. At first sight it might seem that the answer pretty clearly would have to be negative. But on further reflection it seems to me that, even setting aside all assumptions, concerns, and questions which we might think belong to a bygone age, there are two ideas we should not throw out without giving them further thought.

The first idea is this. Clearly, the Stoics think we shall not understand human beings unless we assume not only that they are guided in what they do by what they take to be the truth but also that they are constructed in a way that makes them highly sensitive to the truth. That is to say, they are pretty good at discriminating what is true and in understanding why it is true. Hence the Stoics believe that ideally we would be guided in what we do not just by what we take to be the truth but by our knowledge and understanding of what the world is actually like, by what the truth actually is. What stands in the way of this, according to the Stoics, are the false beliefs and misguided attitudes which we individually have about things. Because of these failings we make choices which are not solely determined by the actual truth about the world but in good part by our false beliefs and our misguided attitudes. It seems fair to say that the Stoic notion of a free will is the notion of an ability to make choices which are responsive to how things are, not distorted by false beliefs and misguided attitudes or by fantasies and wishful thinking. This idea does not seem hopeless.

The second idea is this. The Stoics believe, just like Aristotle and, I take it, Plato, that there is no closed set of general rules or truths such that, if only you knew them, you could deduce from them the right thing to do in any given situation.[18] What there is consists, in principle, of an open set of general truths, of which you may know any number. In a given situation the number you know will suffice to determine what is the right thing to do. So in this sense the situation will not pose a problem. But, because the set in principle is open, you may often, if you are wise, get into a situation where the relevant truths you know do not suffice to enable you to make a choice which does justice to the situation. Nevertheless the wise person will make the right choice. And he will be able to explain this choice in a way which will satisfy any reasonable person by adding to the set of general truths which guide his behavior some further truth or truths, thus enriching the repertory of relevant considerations. Solving the problem he is facing in this way requires precisely the kind of ingenuity, creativity, thoughtfulness, and insight which the Stoic wise person wants to display in his actions, in imitation of God. And this idea, that a will is free if it can make such choices, does not seem to me to be hopeless, either.

CHAPTER SIX

Platonist and Peripatetic Criticisms and Responses

If we now look at how the Stoic notion of a free will was received by the Stoics' contemporaries, we might think that, given the massive assumptions involved, it would not have much chance to be accepted at all. But it turns out that Christians just after the time of Epictetus were beginning to articulate their beliefs in what they themselves often thought of, and called, a new philosophy. For the most part they found these assumptions highly congenial. Almost immediately, with some modifications they adopted the Stoic notion of a free will. There is no doubt that the belief in a free will became so widespread, indeed for a long time almost universal, thanks to the influence of Christianity.

But we shall have occasion to consider this in detail when we discuss Origen and Augustine. For now I will restrict myself to a consideration of the Stoics' main philosophical rivals, the Platonists and the Peripatetics. They were prepared to accept, as we have seen, a notion of a will. They were also prepared to accept a notion of freedom and, with a great deal more hesitation, the language of a free will. But they were not prepared to accept many of the assumptions which went with this notion in Stoicism. So these rivals had at best a highly modified notion of a free will. The main stumbling block was the Stoic doctrine of fate and an all-encompassing divine providence, or, as we regularly put the matter, the Stoic assumption of a universal determinism.

To understand the ensuing dispute we have to go back a long time before there was any notion of a free will. The dispute started as a debate about whether it can be said that our actions are up to us *(eph' hēmin)*, or in our power, if they, like everything else which happens in the world, are determined by fate. And for the most part it continued to be a debate about this point. But the Stoics' opponents completely disregarded the distinctive features of Stoic determinism, treating it as if it were the kind of determinism Epicurus had rejected (see p. 12). In particular, they paid no attention to the probably Chrysippean distinction between an action which is free *(autopragia)*, and an action which, though not free, we are still responsible for because it was up to us to do it or not to do it and which depended for its getting done on our being this sort of person.

Presumably, the opponents disregarded these particular features of Stoic determinism, because they all rejected universal determinism as such, and so the particular form in which it came did not seem to matter much. Also, the particular features of Stoic determinism are so tied up with specifically Stoic beliefs, which the opponents would reject anyway, that they saw little reason to pay particular attention to them. Finally, because the Stoics themselves admitted that there are practically no wise people, the distinction between free actions and forced actions, which we are nevertheless responsible for, seemed rather academic. For all practical purposes the Stoics seemed to claim that, though our actions (inasmuch as we are fools) are not free but forced by fate through the external objects of our desire, we are nevertheless responsible for these actions. That is because, being the people we have become, we gave assent to the corresponding impressions. The opponents found this objectionable.

They argued that it was a misuse of the notions of "up to us" *(eph' hēmin)* or "in our power" *(in nostra potestate)* to apply them to cases where our assent is forced. And they claimed that this Stoic sense of "up to us" was too weak to justify attribution of responsibility to a person. For how can a person be held responsible for something the person is forced to do?

We can already see which direction the debate was bound to take. The opponents of the Stoics would try to specify a stronger notion of what is up to us, which in their view would justify our attribution of responsibility to a person. But in the end, to elucidate their notion of a responsible action, they would introduce notions of freedom, free action, and free will, which in one sense are much weaker than the corresponding, incredibly strong, Stoic notions.

If we try to trace the debate, we can follow it from Carneades' time, that is, the middle of the second century B.C.[1] It needs to be said, though, that our evidence concerning this debate is extremely meager until we come to Alexander of Aphrodisias at the end of the second century A.D. Our main piece of evidence for Carneades and the intervening period is Cicero's short work *De fato,* which, moreover, is extant only in a highly mutilated form. On the evidence of Cicero, it seems that Carneades tried to do precisely what the opponents had to do, namely, give a new, alternative account of what it is for something to be up to us, which made this a stronger notion.

In considering Carneades' account, we have to keep in mind

that he was an Academic skeptic, and that the kind of Academic skepticism he espoused excludes the possibility that he himself endorsed his account. This was part of a dialectical argument to neutralize whatever inclination one may have to accept the Stoic account and so was offered as an equally viable alternative. According to Cicero (XI. 23), Carneades criticized Epicurus for introducing a motion without a cause, namely, the swerve of the atoms. In common parlance, Carneades argues, we do say that something happens without a cause or even that somebody wants something or does not want something without a cause. But this is just a manner of speaking. What we mean is that there is no external antecedent cause for what one is doing. This does not mean that there is no cause at all. There is always a cause. It is just that sometimes the cause is internal. For instance, in the case of atoms it is true that they do not need an external antecedent cause to move, let us say, something which gives them a push; rather, they can move all by themselves. But this motion, when they move by themselves, is not without a cause and explanation altogether. The cause lies in the nature of the atom, which is such that the atom can move by itself, on account of its weight. And, Carneades continues, according to Cicero (XI. 25), there similarly are voluntary motions of the soul. These are not motions which have their explanation in some antecedent external cause but in some internal cause.

Now, given the analogy of the atoms, Cicero is surely wrong when he identifies this internal cause as the nature of these voluntary motions. Given the analogy of the atoms, Carneades must have said that these voluntary motions have their origin in the nature of the soul or the organism. It is easy to see what his point must have been. The nature of the soul or the organism is such that, if the organism is depleted, it will want to have something to eat or drink and hence will go to look for something to eat or drink. If, on the other hand, the organism is satiated, it naturally will not want to have something to eat or drink, and, accordingly, it will not go out to look for something. So the organism's or the soul's wanting to have something to eat and its going to get something to eat are not due to any external antecedent cause, an appetizing object out there, which makes it want to have something to eat.

In trying to interpret these remarks, we should not be misled by Cicero's term *motus voluntarii*. This expression does not refer to a will, let alone a free will, which causes these motions. For we are told what causes them: the nature of the soul or the organism. If they are called voluntary (I presume the Greek would be *hekousioi*), it is because they are not produced by an external, antecedent cause and in this sense forced on us. They are produced by the nature of the organism. And they are in that sense up to us (see Cicero's expression *in nostra potestate*). If we need something to eat, our nature is such that we will want to have something to eat and will go and get something to eat; if we do not need something to eat, our nature is such that we will not want to have something to eat, and we will not move.[2]

But, to return to Carneades, having a rough idea of his dialectical position, we next have to see how this is supposed to constitute a challenge to Chrysippus's view. The way we have characterized the Stoic view, as described in Cicero's *De fato* and the way Carneades will have understood it, is this: An appetizing object is out there; this object is an external, antecedent cause, for it evokes in us an agreeable impression; this too is an antecedent cause, for it evokes in us an assent to the impression; and we are responsible, because, given the sort of person we are, we give assent, whether we can help it or not.

Carneades cleverly shifts the Chrysippean paradigm.[3] Having already, in reference to Epicurus, drawn a clear distinction between forced and natural motions of atoms, he seems to assume similarly that the *motus voluntarii* of the soul or the organism are to be contrasted with forced motions, meaning motions caused by an external antecedent cause. Whereas Chrysippus had said that giving assent to the appropriate impression makes all ensuing actions up to us or in our power, Carneades distinguishes between those actions in which assent is forced and those in which assent has its origin in our nature, namely, those instances in which it is natural for us to want a certain kind of object. He thus considerably restricts the scope of what is *hekousion,* or voluntary, and thereby reduces the scope of what we are responsible for, not only in comparison with Chrysippus but also in comparison with Aristotle. In effect, Carneades allows for psychological compulsion to be exculpating in a way it was not for Aristotle.

In this way Carneades also narrows the notion of what is up to us, in relation to both Aristotle and Chrysippus. When Aristotle had said that you can only choose to do what it is up to you to do or not to do, what he had in mind was simply that in these cases the world is such that it depends entirely on you, is completely in your control, whether something gets done or not done. For this it was entirely irrelevant whether you were or were not under such psychological compulsion that you could not but choose to do what you did. All that mattered was that it would not get done unless you did it. But this is now ruled out by Carneades. For something to be up to you, to be in your power, you must not be under the spell of the object of your desire. And this correspondingly narrows down the notion of a choice. You now have a choice only if you are not compelled to want something. But there is still no sign in Carneades of a notion of a will or a notion of freedom or a notion of free will.

Things are different when we now make a jump and look at Alexander of Aphrodisias at the end of the second century A.D.[4] Both Carneades and Chrysippus, it seems, had regarded the notion of what is up to us and the notion of the voluntary *(hekousion)* as coextensive, except that Carneades had limited both notions by excluding actions done under psychological compulsion. In the case of Alexander, we have a philosopher who can look back on more than two centuries of serious and almost scholastic study of Aristotle by philosophers who regard him as an authority. Aristotle, as we have seen (p. 26), clearly distinguishes between what we do of our own accord *(hekontes)* and what we do by choice, because it is up to us. Hence, of course, Alexander will also insist on this distinction, which non-Peripatetics by now had forgotten and were easily confused about. Thus we find Alexander drawing the distinction in a passage we have looked at before (*De fato* XIV, p. 183, 27ff; see p. 57). But now we should note that he characterizes an action as voluntary *(hekousion)* if it is due to an unforced assent *(abiastos synkatathesis)* to an impression. This is clearly Carneades' notion of the voluntary. Furthermore Alexander proceeds to characterize "what is up to us" *(to eph' hēmin)* more narrowly, as a matter of assent based on a rational evaluation of one's impression. Hence, for Alexander, something's being in our power involves not only, as in Carneades, our assent's not being forced, it also involves a critical scrutiny of our impression.

Alexander's argument against the Stoics crucially relies on the claim that, given their doctrine of fate, they abuse the notion of "what is up to us" by disregarding the fact that, if something is up to us, its happening or not happening cannot already be settled by the state of the world; in this regard they rely on Aristotle's view of choice. But he also argues that, since the Stoics use the notion of "what is up to us" even when assent is forced (as, according to the Stoics, it invariably is, so long as we are fools), they are misusing the expression "up to us" (*De fato* XXXVIII, p. 211, 27ff) and doing away with freedom *(to eleutheron)*. In this connection Alexander repeatedly also uses the term *autexousion*. His treatise almost ends with the remark that a person is in charge *(kyrios)* of only those actions of which he himself *(autos)* also has the power *(exousia)* not to do them. So Alexander explicitly makes freedom a condition for voluntariness and thus for responsibility. In fact, he does so in the sentence referred to in the very terms the Stoics use to define *freedom*. He thereby also makes freedom a condition for what is up to us. This freedom, though, is not the freedom of the Stoics. That freedom presupposes that nothing whatsoever can force one's assent. This is why only the wise man is free and why, as Alexander notes (*De fato* XXVIII, p. 199, 16ff), for the Stoics only one or two people have ever been wise and free. In contrast, Alexander's freedom is of a more limited kind. For him it suffices that over a sufficiently large range of objects which we try to attain or avoid, our action is not compelled by them, and that our assent, in such cases, is not forced.

The notion of freedom involved here is a relative one. To be responsible for going after a certain object of desire, one must be free relative to that object of desire. There is, of course, nothing in the notion of freedom that Alexander is using which would prevent somebody from being free relative to all objects of desire. Then we would have a will which is entirely free in Alexander's sense of *free*. But this is not the Stoic sense of *free*. For in the Stoic sense of *freedom,* any inappropriate attachment would deprive you of freedom altogether. Nevertheless, one might think that Alexander's notion was more realistic in that it allowed for degrees of being free.

What is more problematic is how he tries to give positive content to his notion of freedom. If we are not forced by the object of desire to go after that object, what are we positively free to do? Here again Alexander relies on Aristotle's notion that something is up to us if whether it gets done entirely depends on us.[5] But this claim admits of two interpretations. We already saw in the case of Aristotle that the fact that it is up to you to do or not to do something does not mean that you have a choice. It means that you can choose to do something but can also fail to choose to do it, and failing to choose to do something does not mean that you choose not to do it. Yet Alexander now, in explicating his notion of freedom, seems to understand freedom precisely in this sense: you can choose to do it, and you can also choose not to do it.

In trying to explicate this, Alexander seems to be driven into a hopeless tangle. He is perfectly aware that, according to Aristotle, the virtuous person cannot choose otherwise. This is what it is to be virtuous, to have no trace of a motivation left to act other than virtuously. So Alexander recurs to the fact that there was a point before the virtuous person was virtuous at which he could have chosen otherwise. But this has the consequence that now human freedom, if it involves the ability to choose otherwise, looks like a sign of human weakness, an inference actually drawn by a follower of Alexander's, the author of the *Mantissa* (chapter XXII).[6] It is clear, at least in part, what motivates Alexander's position. He is so eager to reject determinism that he not only wants to reject determinism from the outside in the form of objects which force our assent. He also wants to reject determinism from the inside. And so, prompted by a Stoic claim to the contrary, he is willing to claim that under identical conditions, both internal and external, that is to say, under the same external circumstances and the same internal conditions of the mind, it is still possible to choose and to act otherwise (*De fato* 192, 22ff).[7] Here we have come very close to Dihle's favored notion of a will which decides or chooses in some mysterious way that is independent not only of the external objects of desire but also of the desires and beliefs of the person.[8]

I am inclined to think, though, that Alexander's position is also the result of what I take to be another confusion. Alexander lived in an age in which there was an enormous concern for justice, a concern that each get what he deserves, instead of some getting what they do not deserve and most not getting what they deserve. When we go back to Aristotle, responsibility, praise, blame, reward, and punishment were not a matter of desert in the way this came to be understood later. Aristotle's idea, like Chrysippus's, is clearly that we take somebody to task for what he is doing, because we want to change his motivation. For this purpose it is quite irrelevant how the person came to be thus motivated or whether he could have helped being thus motivated. We have to keep in mind that Aristotle's notion of responsibility also applies to children and to animals. And we surely are not concerned about whether the animal had much choice in doing what it did. We are concerned that it has still not learned its lesson. We do not ask how it came about that it has failed to do so. We give it another lesson. We encourage and discourage animals, children, and grown-ups for as long as it is appropriate. That is no longer appropriate for the person who is wise and virtuous, who has learned his lesson, but this does not mean that we cannot find what the virtuous person is doing quite wonderful and admirable or that his action lacks merit, just because there is no longer any need for encouragement.

When we encourage a child, we are telling the child that it is doing pretty well. By this we mean that it is well on its way to becoming wise and virtuous. Indeed, the child's action is a further step on this road. This is why it has merit. We think that the child for its age is doing admirably. And we think this against the background of what other children of this age in this situation might have done. This does not at all mean that we think that the child's merit lies in the fact that it could also have behaved miserably, as other children might have done, but chose not to behave in this way. It might not even have occurred to the child that it could act otherwise. The merit does not lie in its having made the right choice, when it could have chosen otherwise, let alone in its choice not to act otherwise. The merit lies in its having done remarkably well for a child of this age in this situation, raising expectations about the future. This is why we encourage and reward it.

Just think of a builder who has still not quite mastered the art. Yet the house he has now built is actually pretty good, and so we might praise and reward him. The merit lies in his having done an admirable job for somebody at his stage of mastering the art of building. We are not going to ask whether he could have helped doing this. And we would be positively stunned if he came to ask a reward for having not built a bad house, when he could have chosen to do so.

But the notion Alexander seems to have is precisely this— that there is no merit or demerit in what you are doing, unless you could have acted otherwise, indeed unless you could have chosen to act otherwise. You now earn praise and a reward, because you chose to act in the right way, when you could have chosen to act in the wrong way. And from here it will not be a long step to the completely un-Aristotelian, or un-Platonic, idea that what makes your action so virtuous and praiseworthy is that you did not choose such a tempting and appealing alternative, when it was on offer. Indeed, it seems to be Alexander's view that what is meritorious about the virtuous person's virtue and virtuous action is that it is a product of the meritorious choices the person made earlier in his life, when he could still have chosen otherwise.

This is simply wrong. The merit of the virtuous action lies in the action, the choice which led to it, and the motivation which led to this choice. Any earlier actions have merit to the extent that they show the person to be well on the way towards becoming virtuous. They decidedly do not derive their merit from the fact that at this point the person did not choose to take an alternative course of action when it was open for him to do so.

Hence it seems to me that Alexander's notion of freedom as a matter of being, in the same circumstances, able to act and to choose to act otherwise is due in good part to his mistaken notion of due desert. In any case, it is in Alexander that we find the ancestor of the notion that to have a free will is to be able, in the very same circumstances, to choose between doing A and doing B. Unfortunately, though, but also as we would expect, Alexander is not able to provide a coherent account of how such a free will is supposed to be possible.

Alexander got into this tangle mainly for two reasons. First, he did not sufficiently understand Stoic determinism, so he did not see that a choice might be no less free for having a perfectly good explanation in terms of antecedent causes. The wise person would have to be crazy not to make the choice he does, even though that choice is not impossible. But this does not make his choice unfree. Second, Alexander has a mistaken notion of merit, as if merit were a matter of not choosing to act otherwise.

If somebody does something remarkable, surely the merit lies in the accomplishment, not in the fact that the person could have chosen to do something quite unremarkable instead. If one writes a review of a book, it surely would be misunderstood if one said that the merit of the book lay in the fact that the author, instead of choosing to write this book, could have chosen to spend the time on the beach. We deserve no credit for not being crazy or for not choosing to do crazy things, and we have no reason for complaint, if we are not free to do crazy things.

CHAPTER SEVEN

An Early Christian View on a Free Will: Origen

It is quite striking that, once we move beyond the age of the New Testament and the apostolic fathers, Christian literature soon begins to abound in references to freedom and to a free will. The references are not quite as abundant as a look at translations and commentaries on early Christian literature might make us believe. They often rely on a vague and supposedly ordinary notion of a free will, and they also translate or paraphrase expressions like "what is up to us" in terms of "free will," a phenomenon we have already noticed in the case of how pagan philosophical texts are treated. But even restricting oneself to unambiguous and explicit references to freedom, a free will, or the freedom of the will, one finds them in abundance, beginning slowly in the middle of the second century A.D., but then, by the next century, turning into a torrent. Thus Justin Martyr repeatedly uses the technical term *autexousion* to refer to our freedom.[1] The first person ever, whether pagan or Christian, to use the expression "the freedom of the will" *(eleutheria tēs prohaireseōs)* is Tatian in his *Oratio ad Graecos* (chapter 7.1) in the third quarter of the second century A.D. Thereafter these terms become more and more frequent, relatively much more so, it seems, than in contemporary pagan literature. Obviously, some doctrine of a free will came to matter greatly to Christians. There is no doubt that the notion of a free will found almost universal acceptance owing to the influence of Christianity.

We have to ask ourselves where the Christians got this notion, whether and how they adapted it in certain ways so as to fit their Christian beliefs, and whether those beliefs even allowed them to find or see a radically new way of understanding human beings, human freedom, and the will.

The answer to the first question seems relatively easy. The Christians got their notion of a free will from Platonism and, most of all, from Stoicism. Many of the massive assumptions associated in Stoicism with the doctrine of free will, for instance, the assumption of a universal divine providence and a divine order regulating everything which happens in the world down to the smallest detail, were utterly unacceptable to Peripatetics, acceptable only with serious qualifications by Platonists, but apparently quite congenial to Christians. If we look at scripture in the form of the Septuagint or at the New Testament as it was beginning to evolve, there is no authority for the language of either human freedom or a free will or, so far as I can see, for the assumption of a free will. When, early in the third century A.D., Origen collects passages from scripture to support the doctrine of a free will, all he can find are passages which you might take to imply that there is a free will but only if you already believe that there is such a thing or that God would not order us to do certain things unless we had a free will which allowed us to comply with these commands.[2] Hence the Christian notion of a free will must come from somewhere else. So where does Tatian, for instance, get his notion of it?

At this point we should note that Tatian (ca. A.D. 110–180) must himself have been a philosopher before his conversion.[3] He seems to hint at this, when in the introduction to *Ad Graecos* he says farewell to pagan wisdom, though not without remarking, with a certain satisfaction, that he himself had acquired some reputation for it. [4] Later in his oration he tells us that he had written a book on animals, and a chapter later he seems to refer to a book on daemons.[5] Since in his book on animals he claims to have attacked the view that animals lack reason and intelligence, he cannot have been a Peripatetic or a Stoic. Since he seems to have written a book on daemons, he cannot have been an Epicurean. Hence he must have been a Platonist. This is confirmed by the fact that the closest parallel to his view on animal intelligence is to be found in the second-century Platonist Celsus, against whom Origen wrote his *Contra Celsum*.[6] It also fits the fact that Tatian was a follower of Justin Martyr, who, before his conversion, had been a Platonist and continued after his conversion to present himself as a philosopher, advancing a new Christian philosophy.[7] As I noted earlier, Justin a couple of times refers to human freedom, using the philosophical term *autexousion*. We should also note that the Alexandrian school of Christian theology, from which Origen was to come, had been founded by Pantaenus, who was originally a Stoic philosopher.[8] So it is not surprising that in Origen's famous student, Clement of Alexandria, who was heavily indebted to Pantaenus, there is a good deal of reference to the fact that there are things which it is up to us *(to eph' hēmin)* to do or not to do. It is noteworthy, though, that the discussion in Clement is still in terms of that well-worn philosophical expression.

Origen is important to my argument for several reasons. First, because, as we shall study shortly, he has a good deal to say about freedom and the free will. He even has a small treatise on the subject, as part of his great and ambitious work *De principiis,* which unfortunately is extant in its entirety only in a Latin translation by Rufinus.[9] I presume, in fact, that Origen was the first Christian author ever to write in detail and systematically about the free will.

Second, Origen himself had had training as a philosopher. He presumably had been a student of Ammonius Saccas, who had also been the teacher of Plotinus.[10] According to Eusebius (*HE* VI.I.I), Origen enjoyed a considerable reputation among philosophers. Porphyry seems to have been familiar with his work and even claimed to have known him. In any case, Porphyry supposedly could find no fault with Origen's doctrines but found it all the more puzzling and disingenuous how Origen could be a Christian and claim to find these doctrines in barbarian scripture, when they so obviously had their source in Greek philosophy.[11] We also know from Gregory Thaumaturgus's *Panegyricus* (xiii) that Origen instructed his students in philosophy.[12] Part of Origen's program was to develop a theory about the world which, while remaining faithful to the fundamental tenets of Christianity, would make them intelligible and rationally acceptable and moreover would answer all the questions a reasonable Christian would have which had not yet been settled by the doctrine of the church. Origen, as far as I can tell, constitutes an enormous advance in the detail, systematism, and sophistication with which questions of Christianity were dealt. All future theology would owe him a great debt, though this was rarely acknowledged. Already in Origen's lifetime his ambitious speculations, with their obvious source in Platonism, frightened some church authorities. It helped little that he was a man of singular piety, who died a confessor and was defended in writing by as unquestionable an authority as Pamphilius. Thus Gregory of Nyssa, who was only too aware of his indebtedness to Origen, both in the conversion of his family by Origen's student Gregory Thaumaturgus and also in theology, carefully avoids mentioning Origen except in one or two places.

Third, even Origen's fiercest critics, like Methodius, could find no fault with his views on the free will.[13] In fact, these views gained an authoritative status from the fact that Basil of Caesarea, Gregory of Nyssa's brother, and Gregory the Theologian, that is, Gregory of Nazianzus, in their *Philocalia* (chapters 21 to 27) anthologized the little treatise on the free will, or, rather, on freedom, from the beginning of book III of the *De principiis,* thus preserving the original Greek version of the text for us.[14] They also excerpted other texts by Origen bearing on the doctrine of a free will, for instance, a passage from the *Contra Celsum,* another from the *Commentary on Genesis,* and yet another from the *Commentary on the Letter to the Romans.* Since Basil and Gregory the Theologian accepted these texts as useful reading on our questions about the free will, we have to assume that they took them to reflect Christian orthodoxy on the matter. Hence we may treat Origen's position as fairly representative of the Christian position in the East in the third and fourth centuries A.D., though I have to quickly add that some of the inferences Origen drew from his doctrine of free will were already opposed by them and came to be anathematized later.

We get a measure of the importance Origen attributes to the doctrine of a free will, if we see that in the *Commentary on John* (ad XIII.19.12.16) he tells us that, as Christians, we have to believe in our God, in Jesus Christ, in the Holy Spirit, and in the fact that we will be punished or rewarded according to the way we have lived, because we are free *(eleutheroi)*.[15] It should strike us as curious that belief in human freedom as the presupposition of divine punishment and reward should take fourth place after belief in God, Jesus Christ, and the Holy Spirit. But this is not a slip on Origen's part. For in the preface to *De principiis*, 4–5, we are similarly told that there are certain basic truths about which apostolic teaching does not leave any room for doubt or lack of clarity. The list of these truths, which any theory will have to accommodate, begins thus: (1) there is one God; (2) Christ is born of the Father; (3) there is the Holy Spirit; and (4) the soul has a life of its own: it will be punished or rewarded, according to its desert, but also any rational soul is endowed with a free will.

I want to add quickly, for those who are not interested in Christian fundamental tenets, that, as far as my brief paraphrase of Origen's list is concerned, many a pagan Platonist in Origen's time would have gladly subscribed to some of its items. What matters, though, for our purposes is that the assumption of a free will is again presented as one of the most fundamental parts of the teaching of the church. We should also note, however, that in the *De principiis* III.i.i, at the very outset of the treatise on free will, Origen expresses himself much more carefully. It becomes clear from Origen's remarks there that, while it is a crucial part of the church's teaching that we will be judged, and judged justly, he himself is inferring that we must therefore assume our freedom; for otherwise we could not be made responsible for what we have done, at least not if God's judgment is just, as we have to take it to be. This assumption that responsibility presupposes freedom or even a free will, of course, is not new. We have encountered it in Alexander of Aphrodisias, and we find it already in Tatian. Nevertheless it is remarkable with what ease it is made by Origen. The belief in a free will would be officially recognized as church doctrine by a synod in Carthage only at the beginning of the fifth century.

Here, then, we have one reason why Origen is so interested in the doctrine of freedom and a free will. A crucial part of the doctrine of the church is that we will be punished or rewarded for our deeds, and he takes it as obvious that this presupposes our freely choosing to act in this way.

There is another, less obvious reason why freedom is so important for Origen. He believes that the world as we know it, though created by God, is a result of the use which rational creatures have made of the freedom with which God endowed them when he created them after his image. God originally created free intellects or minds, all of which were equal.[16]

At this point we may wonder what disembodied intellects use a will for. Here we should remember the complex Stoic notion of a will as an ability to make choices and decisions, that is, not just choices to give assent to impulsive impressions (to will to do something) but choices to give assent to impressions quite generally. Even disembodied intellects do something: they think. This is what they already do in Plato and Aristotle. Hence they have thoughts or impressions, and they have to choose which ones to give assent to and which ones not to give assent to. This, though, presupposes that they do not already know everything. And this, indeed, is what Origen does assume. It is perhaps not entirely clear why he assumes it. To understand his point we have to take note that what there is to know for the intellects is God, themselves, and the other intellects. To know God is to know the Trinity, and to know the Trinity is to know the Father, that is to say, the Good; the Son, that is to say, the divine intellect and hence eternal truth; and the Holy Spirit. So there is a great deal to know.

There is one notorious problem here for any Platonist. Plato in the *Republic* (6.509b) had claimed that the Good is transcendent: it is beyond being and the intellect, since it is the source of all being and all intelligibility and hence not itself a being and intelligible. Therefore God, or at least God the Father, being the Good, is transcendent and hence beyond the intellectual understanding of even the purest intellect.[17] Nevertheless there must be some kind of understanding of the Good, if it is also true that everything is supposed to be understood in terms of the Good as the first principle. This is a kind of understanding which the Platonists have in mind when they talk about the different ways in which one may come to understand God, however inadequately, for instance, by negative theology. So the created intellects are not omniscient, not only in the ordinary sense that they do not know everything but also in the deeper sense that there is something which, in principle, they cannot know at all but only understand more or less adequately on the basis of what they know.

On the other hand, we have to presume that they are created with some knowledge, since otherwise they would not be in a position to think about things at all. So they will have inborn notions which incorporate a basic knowledge of reality of the kind Plato, Aristotle, and the Stoics ascribe to anybody who has reason. So they are created free, with this knowledge, which enables them to advance in their understanding and to get a better grasp of God or the Good, if they properly put their minds to it.[18] Now the more they advance in their understanding of the Good, the more their minds will be a reflection of God and the more they will be like God, in the way an image in a nondistorting mirror can be like the object seen in it. Plato in the *Theaetetus* (176b) had claimed that the end of life consists in becoming like

God *(homoiōsis theōi).* This is taken up by Platonists in the imperial period as the formula for what we should aim at in life. And this is also what Origen believes and how he interprets it. But, I take it, Origen also believes himself to be following scripture when it says that man is created in the image and in the likeness *(homoiōsis)* of God.[19] Man is created as a free intellect so that he can become as like God as is possible for a creature. Now, as the intellect gets a better understanding of the Good, and the more clearly one sees it, the Good seems ever more attractive, and this constitutes an ever stronger motivation to understand it and become like it.

But this, of course, presupposes that one proceeds with great care and diligence in these difficult matters, so as to give assent only to impressions or thoughts which deserve it; for one may at some point lack attention or care and give assent to a false thought. This immediately has the consequence of blurring one's view of the truth, and hence one's ability to see the Good, however minute the blur might be. Once error has crept in, it is more difficult not to make further mistakes. And as the mistakes pile up, one's view of the truth gets seriously distorted, one's understanding of the Good seriously tainted, and as a result the Good seems less and less attractive. Metaphorically speaking, instead of rising upwards, one sinks downwards.

I have gone into this in some detail, because we shall need the detail later. But what we need for the moment is Origen's view that these intellects, which are created equal, through their own behavior and the use of their will to give assent or refuse to give assent, fall into various degrees of error. In this way the intellects come to be separated into a hierarchy of angels, human souls, and daemons. Origen assumes, moreover, that God anticipated this fall, and therefore created the visible world with bodies, so that human souls, when embodied, might be able to undo the consequences their mistakes had had on their minds. This has the result that the whole material world, as we know it, including the visible world, is contingent on the free will of creatures.[20]

These ideas have an important bearing on the meaning of the title of Origen's treatise. It has been suggested that the title might refer to the principles of reality, the principles in terms of which reality is to be understood.[21] This seems to me to be almost certainly right. The title *Peri archōn* is a typical title for Platonist treatises on the principles of reality. We know of such works by Longinus and Porphyry, and we still have Damascius's *On Principles*. This is how Marcellus of Ancyra understood Origen's title, when he criticized Origen for not first having studied scripture sufficiently but having instead turned to writing on sacred matters by relying on the works of the Platonists, as Marcellus supposed to be evident already from the mere title. Eusebius responded to this criticism not by claiming that Origen's title had nothing to do with these Platonist treatises but by denying that the word *principles* in any way contradicts the assumption that there is one ultimate principle, the Father.[22] This understanding of Origen's title makes all the more sense once we see that in Origen's view the world is intelligible only by being, in some sense, the product of the freedom of creatures. Conversely, this understanding of the title underlines the importance Origen attributes to freedom and the free will. It is, after the Trinity, the next most important principle.

At this point we should take a brief look at Origen's short treatise "On Freedom" *(Peri autexousiou)* in *De princ.* III.1. As I have already said, Origen begins by pointing out that we shall be judged justly for what we did, and punished or rewarded accordingly, and that this obviously presupposes that we are free, meaning that it is up to us and depends on us *(eph' hēmin)* whether or not we do the things which merit praise or vituperation. Origen here simply identifies freedom with there being things which are up to us to do or not to do. So by the end of III.1.1 he announces that he is first going to set out the notion of what is up to us and then, on the basis of having explicated this notion, clarify matters. Accordingly, in III.1.2–3 he sets out the notion of what it is for there to be things which are up to us.

This explication proceeds along standard Stoic lines. And, on the basis of this, in III.1.4–5, first part, he argues that somebody who maintains that he could not help but act the way he does, because the external circumstances make him act the way he does (for instance, in the form of an attractive woman), obviously has not understood what it is for something to be up to us. Such a person has a deviant notion of freedom, because he thinks one is free to do things to the extent that one can do what one intends to do, if the circumstances do not provoke one into doing something else (III.1.5).

Origen dutifully points out that all the circumstances can do is produce an impression in you to which you can refuse to assent, though you can also, because of its titillating coloring, assent to it. In III.1.5, second part, he briefly turns to the possibility that somebody might argue that he is not to blame for what he is doing, because, given his congenital or natural constitution *(kataskeuē)*, he cannot act otherwise than he does. Again Origen dutifully points out that many people have managed to overcome their congenital dispositions. By III.1.6 he turns to the scriptural passages which are supposed to confirm freedom, and at III.1.7–24 he finally comments on scriptural passages which might be taken to show that we are not free in our actions or even in our decisions.

At first sight all this seems rather disappointing, especially if we had expected some new views about freedom and the free will. The systematic account at the outset could have been taken straight from a late Stoic handbook. We do not even learn from this little treatise that for Origen freedom *(to autexousion)* is a matter of having a free will *(prohairesis eleuthera).* For this we have to turn to other parts of the *De principiis* and other writings of Origen.[23] The terminology and the claims, with the exception of our crucial implicit claim, are through and through Stoic, with the terminology almost invariably being found in Epictetus and almost all the major claims having their parallels in him, too. Some of Origen's explications of scriptural texts become intelligible only against the background of the kind of theory we have ascribed to Epictetus. Hence one thing is obvious: Origen is very heavily relying on the late Stoic doctrine of free will; if there is some deviation from it, Origen's remarks on freedom are certainly not meant to be directed against the Stoics to put them right.

Nevertheless it is pretty clear that Origen's remarks are directed against opponents. After all, the very point of the *De principiis,* as the preface says, is to clarify certain fundamental matters which are not settled by apostolic teaching but about which there is disagreement or controversy among those who profess to believe in Jesus Christ. Note the language "profess to believe" *(se credere profitentur).*[24] This suggests that Origen is relying on a basically Stoic doctrine of a free will to criticize certain, in his view, heterodox views which many Christians hold or at least are tempted by. I want to argue that these views are astral determinism and various forms of what we now call "Gnosticism," though for Origen himself the "Gnostics" were just one particular group among them (see *CC* 5.61).

Here we have to keep in mind that the doctrine of the church emerged slowly, starting in about A.D. 150, and only became fully defined centuries later. We also need to keep in mind that what, by the light of later centuries, would count as orthodox mainstream Christianity was pretty fluid even in Origen's day and had been even more so before his time. In the second century both Valentinus and Marcion could live for many years as members of the church in Rome before being expelled.[25] We have to remember too that when lines were drawn, the various Gnostic groups, as we learn, for instance, from Tertullian's *In Hermogenem,* managed to draw large numbers of Christians to their side. Even in Origen's day, then, large numbers of Christians were Gnostics even within the church, members of the church were tempted by Gnosticism, and the schismatic Gnostics had to be persuaded to return to the truth. In one form or another Gnosticism continued to be a threat to the church for a long time.

Also astral determinism, to be distinguished from the view that the constellation of the stars is a sign of what is to come (a view shared by the Stoics and Origen), proved to be as attractive to Christians as to non-Christians.[26] Sometimes, in fact, as in the *Apocryphon of John,* astral determinism was part of a Gnostic view of the world.[27] As we can see from the church fathers (for instance, Eusebius, Gregory of Nyssa, or Augustine), astral determinism continued to be tempting to Christians for a long time to come. Augustine in a sermon tells us that many hesitate to convert to Christianity because of their astrological beliefs.[28] We can see how seriously Origen took this view because he refers to it in his preface to *De principiis* (5) as a view incompatible with the church's teaching that we are free and also because in his *Commentary on Genesis* he attacked it in some detail. It is a measure of the importance the church continued to attribute to this point that Basil and Gregory Nazianzus also incorporated this text in their *Philocalia* as part of the section on freedom.[29]

Once we see this background, many of the details of Origen's view on freedom and a free will, and also many of the details of his little treatise on freedom, appear in a new light. It immediately becomes clear why nearly four-fifths of this rather short text is taken up by a discussion of scriptural passages which seem to deny a free will, some of the most difficult ones coming from St. Paul, especially the *Letter to the Romans*. Obviously, these were the texts that Origen's Gnostic opponents were relying on. Let us look at this in sufficient detail to convince ourselves that Origen's views on freedom were shaped by these opponents.

Like the Stoics, he believes that the world down to its smallest details is governed by divine providence. But for him there is the troubling fact that human beings are born with very different endowments, or natural constitutions, and that they are born into very different circumstances. Indeed, the congenital constitution and the circumstances may be such that it will be exceedingly difficult, if not impossible, to follow God's orders or commandments. As we have seen, this does not bother Aristotle, but it has to concern Origen because he believes in divine providence and a fair and just God who is omnipotent. Hence God cannot have set up the world in such a way that some (if not most) human beings find it difficult, or even impossible, to follow God's commands.

Origen's solution to this problem, as we have already seen, is to assume that God created all human beings entirely equal, with entirely equal abilities and possibilities as free intellects. He can thus claim that all further differentiations and differences in our destiny, including our physical constitution and the circumstances into which we are born, are the product of our own choices, the self-inflicted punishment which God, in his providence, has arranged to take the particular form it does, because it will thus allow us to remedy the particular defects which brought about our fall (see *De princ.* II.9.6). But we can see from *De princ.* II.9.5 and I.8.2 that others drew a very different conclusion from the agreed fact that we are born with very different natural constitutions and in very different circumstances, which might be exceedingly difficult to deal with, and that Origen is addressing these opponents. In II.9.5 he notes that the followers of Marcion, Valentinus, and Basilides (all important Gnostic heresiarchs) object to the view that a God who is just and good *(aequissimus)* could create people of different natures or natural constitutions and create angels of different orders. They also object, as far as rational creatures here on Earth are concerned, that a good God would not have arranged for human beings to be born under such radically different circumstances which make such a difference to the life they can live. In I.8.2 Origen's opponents argue that it does not make any sense to think that a single creator would create rational beings with different kinds of natures. Origen wholeheartedly agrees with them. But whereas he concludes from this that God created all rational beings equal and that the differences between them are of their own doing, his opponents infer that at least some rational creatures are the work of an inferior creator.

It is pertinent to note here that Origen, early in the preface to *De principiis,* in the second paragraph, explains that the disagreements among those who profess to be Christians do not just concern small and trivial matters but fundamental matters such as God, Jesus Christ, the Holy Spirit, and also certain creatures, namely, the powers *(dominationes)* and sacred virtues *(virtutes sacrae),* according to Rufinus's translation (for this part of

the text we do not have the Greek original). It is these disagreements that the *De principiis* is primarily meant to shed light on
or to resolve.

What Origen must be thinking of here are Gnostic views.[30]
In any case the dispute seems to be about the nature and origin
of certain spiritual beings, regarded by Origen as the angels created by God through Christ but regarded by different Gnostics
in a variety of different ways.[31] The point which matters is that
it is a dispute with the Gnostics. And it is, as we have already
seen, the Gnostics who are in disagreement about the Father of
Jewish scripture who created the world we live in. According to
them, he cannot be good and just and hence cannot be God. The
disagreement about Christ at this point must still be a disagreement with Gnostics. For in Gnostic systems Christ too is a fairly
subordinate being who is sent to save us but who is far removed
from being the mind of God through which God created this
world.

With this we can return to the question of why Gnosticism
raised such big problems concerning the freedom of the will.
Here I want to say from the outset that I am not concerned to
identify the truth about the Gnostic positions Origen attacks.
What matters is that Origen understands them in a certain way,
though I want to add that I give great weight to the evidence
which Origen has to offer on Gnosticism. If we now return to
our short treatise on freedom, we note that two paragraphs,
III.1.4 and 5, separate Origen's explication of what it is for there
to be things which are up to us and his discussion of biblical
passages. These two paragraphs seem at first to deal with two
lame excuses for one's actions. One is that, given one's natural
constitution, one cannot but act in the way one does; the other,
that the circumstances or objects of desire in one's surroundings

make one act the way one does. But it becomes clear, given the Gnostic background, that this must be related to the Gnostic complaint that a good God would never create human beings with such a physical constitution or expose them to such circumstances which make failure predictable. In fact, Origen must mean to answer the view he attributes to Marcion, Valentinus, and Basilides in *De princ.* II.9.5, that human beings have by birth different natures, such that some are essentially good and hence will be saved and some are essentially evil and hence will be damned. Similarly, in *CC* V.61, Origen reports the view, which he now more specifically attributes to the Valentinians, that there are human beings who are spiritual and human beings who are psychic in their constitution and that these beings are saved or lost depending on their natural constitution. In reporting this here, as in *De princ.* III.1.5, he uses the same term, *kataskeuē,* for constitution. We also know of a Gnostic view according to which there are three constitutions, a carnal, a psychic, and a spiritual one, of which the first guarantees damnation, the last salvation, whereas the psychic constitution at least allows one to escape from damnation.

When Origen in III.1.4–5 attacks the view that external objects might have such power over one that one is forced to act in the way one does, he must be responding to the claim that the circumstances into which one is put by the ruler of this visible world in which we live may force us to act otherwise than we should. It is telling how Origen at the beginning of III.1.6 introduces the discussion of the scriptural passages in a way which might as well serve as a summary of the preceding discussion: it should be clear that it is our task *(ergon)* to live well, and God expects this from us, as this is not his task, nor will it come about through the agency of somebody or something else nor, as some believe, through fate. So our life is not determined by God or by any other power or force which might set us up in a certain way nor by fate as, for instance, the determination of the astral powers.

With this we can turn to take at least a brief look at the scriptural passages which put a free will into question and at Origen's treatment of these. Let us consider the following two passages (III.1.7): "It is not a matter of somebody's willing *(thelontos)* or somebody's striving, but of God's mercy" *(Rom.* 9.16), and "both the willing *(thelein)* and the doing come from God" *(Phil.* 2.13). One might well interpret these passages as saying that all things which happen in the world, including our own actions, are the work of God or at least do not come about without his mercy. But they also seem to be saying that our willing is not ours but God's, who at best in his mercy will arrange things in such a way that some of us will make the right choices. One readily understands how these passages could be relied upon by somebody who wanted to argue that our life is a function of the physical constitution which we have been given or the circumstances to which we have been exposed, or both. Discussing the first passage in III.1.18, Origen explicitly says that his opponents adduce it to show that our salvation does not depend on there being things which it is up to us to do or not to do, that is, on our freedom, but on the physical constitution with which we have been created or on the will *(prohairesis)* of him who, if he wills, will have mercy and providentially arrange our life so as to be saved.

The way Origen in response interprets these passages again reflects his indebtedness to Stoicism. He is quite prepared to say that the doing in some important sense in any case is God's, part of the providential unfolding of the course the world takes. Hence, if a house is finally built or if a captain manages to steer his ship through a bad storm into a safe harbor, this in some sense really is God's doing. But Origen is quite uncompromising about the will. Rather implausibly, he declares that Paul must mean that we owe our will to God but cannot mean that each particular willing is due to God.

I take it, then, that Origen integrates a rather detailed, but basically Stoic, view of freedom into his otherwise Platonist outlook on the world, because this Stoic view ideally provides more or less ready answers to a variety of views which Origen and mainstream Christianity later found unorthodox but also particularly threatening. If we briefly go back to Tatian's sparse remarks, we can see that these views must already have been his concern.[32] For Tatian insists that only God is good by nature or essentially. Hence no human being is essentially good and hence bound to be saved. According to Tatian, we have received the freedom of the will to attain the perfection possible for a human being. Therefore no human being is essentially evil by his natural constitution and bound to be damned. Whether we are saved or damned depends on what we do, on the use we make of our freedom. And Tatian immediately proceeds to reflect on the kind of fatalism or determinism which would stand in the way of our being able to do what we need to do in order to be saved.

My claim is that Christianity's interest in freedom and a free will was motivated by a concern with various forms of Gnosticism and astral determinism, that a basically Stoic view on a free will admirably served the purpose of combating these unorthodox views, and that we therefore have no particular reason to expect a radically new notion of a free will's emerging from Christianity.[33]

This, though, is not at all to say that Origen's doctrine of a free will was just the Stoic doctrine. There are important differences. Perhaps we best begin with the one we noted earlier. Origen, unlike Chrysippus and Epictetus, but like Alexander, identifies freedom *(to autexousion)* with there being things which are up to you to do or not to do, that is to say, things such that you are responsible for doing them. He does not think that freedom is something we would naturally have if nothing went wrong with our development, and which we lose the moment we take a wrong step. For Origen we are free from the moment we are created, and this freedom is part of our nature as rational beings, such that we can never lose it. Even the daemons or the devil retain a free will. Thus in particular for Origen the smallest mistake does not have the disastrous consequences it has for the Stoics. For the Stoics all sins are equal, because they are, at least in classical Stoicism, always one and the same sin in the end, namely, giving one's assent to an impression which does not merit assent. For Origen mistakes have their effect in general by accumulation. You can be an angel, make a mistake, and still remain an angel.[34]

There is another important difference between the Stoic notion of freedom and Origen's notion which goes with what I have just said. In Stoicism the person who is wise and has liberated himself from all inappropriate desires and attachments can never make a mistake. There is nothing left in his motivation which could account for his going wrong. He unshakably knows what the good is, and in light of this he acts as wisely, given his limited knowledge, as he can be expected to act. But Origen's created free intellects do not unshakably know the good. They are cognitively separated from it by a gap which can never be completely filled, which may get smaller, as it may get bigger, but never disappears. Hence Origen's intellects can make mistakes, however far they have advanced in wisdom. There is never a state, as in Stoicism, in which there is no possibility of a mistake, and with it as a consequence there is always the possibility of a fall. The other side of the same medal is that the daemons never lose their free will and the knowledge with which they were created. This suffices for them to free themselves from their daemonic qualities and to return ultimately to an angelic status.

This is Origen's famous doctrine of the *apokatastasis*, which for orthodox Christians became an anathema, although none other than Gregory of Nyssa also espoused it in his *De anima et resurrectione*.[35] In fact, it seems that Origen's view was at least sometimes that the ascent and descent of rational beings went on forever. It has to be said that this doctrine could easily undermine the central importance of the redemption as a unique historical event. We can see what later Christians had to do doctrinally to stop this never-ending ascent and descent, to make sure that the damned remain damned forever and the blessed enjoy eternal bliss. We can see it most clearly in Augustine. It is the grace of perseverance which allows the blessed not to fall again, and similarly God declines to continue to extend his grace to those who have fallen forever, without which they could not recover. Indeed, Origen himself already offers the view in *De principiis* I.3.8 that God by his grace may arrange things in such a way that one eternally retains the virtue and wisdom one has attained.

In any case it is true that Origen's view of freedom is not quite the Stoic view. There are important differences. But these do not seem to have their source in Origen's Christianity. They presumably derive from his Platonism, a Platonism heavily indebted in this regard to Stoicism. With this in mind let us look again at how Origen explains the fall of the intellect.

In the *De principiis* he mentions three possible explanations which, I take it, are not supposed to compete with one another. The first is satiety.[36] The intellect has had enough of contemplating the truth, of toiling to distinguish the true from the false among its thoughts (*De princ.* I.3.8). The second explanation is carelessness or negligence (in Rufinus's translation, *neglegentia*); one does not attend sufficiently to one's impressions and carelessly gives assent (I.4.1). The third is laziness *(desidia et laboris taedium,* II.9.2); one has had enough of all the toil involved in always being concerned with the good: again one seems not to show the required diligence and enthusiasm in considering what to take to be true and good. So the will makes the wrong choices. But note the explanation given for these choices. Or, rather, first of all note that an explanation is given.

The choice of the will is not a sheer act of volition with no cause or explanation. The wrong choice is explained as due to lack of the appropriate care. And also note the nature of the choice. You choose to assent when, if you had been more careful, you would not have assented. The choice is not even represented as a choice between two things. For not to choose to give assent to a thought is not at all the same thing as choosing to assent to the contradictory thought. That you refuse to believe that "p" does not mean that you decide to believe that "not p." It is also not the case that the intellect, at least at these early stages of its descent, has the resources to decide to believe something altogether different. So there is nothing mysterious about Origen's will. It is an ability to make the right choices. But we have this ability at a price. The price is that if we do not exercise the required care in making choices, we may fail to make the right choices, fail to give assent when we should, or give assent when we should not. But there is an explanation of why this happens: our carelessness, laziness, satiety. And there is an explanation for this, too.

According to Christians and also according to Origen, everything which is created is subject to change, indeed liable to pass away. This is just a version of the ancient philosophical doctrine that everything which comes into being is subject to change and will pass away. Plato in the *Timaeus* modified this doctrine for the purposes of his creation myth, which many in antiquity, among them, the Platonists Plutarch and Atticus, believed to reflect his own real view. According to this story, God decrees that everything which he himself has created (and this includes the rational part of the soul) will, though by its nature destructible, never pass away.[37] This is an act of divine grace. However, Plato's doctrine as so understood led to considerable confusion in late antiquity, even among Christians, concerning the nature of the soul's immortality.

In any case, Origen's intellects, including their will, are subject to change. This is just a consequence of their being created. And so Origen in *De princ.* I.6.2 points out that these intellects, because it is not part of their nature to be good, as they are not God, sooner or later, to a greater or lesser degree, will cease, if only momentarily, to pay attention to Truth and the Good. But Plato's move in the *Timaeus* indicates the remedy. God by his grace could preserve us not only in our existence but also in our unfailing concern for Truth and the Good. So the question arises of why God does not do this. The orthodox Christian answer is that in this case there would be no merit on our part for which we would earn this grace. Whether this is also Origen's answer depends in good part on whether one assumes that he did believe in a final *apokatastasis*—a state in which all rational creatures have been saved and will be preserved in this blessed state—or whether one thinks that Origen really thought that all intellects descend and ascend forever.

CHAPTER EIGHT

Reactions to the Stoic Notion of a Free Will: Plotinus

GREEK PHILOSOPHICAL AND JUDAEO-CHRISTIAN CONCEPTIONS OF GOD

It is often supposed that traditional versions of the notion of the will were made historically possible only by the Judaeo-Christian conception of God with its emphasis on God's will and its absolute, unconditioned character.[1] This Judaeo-Christian conception is supposed to differ radically from the Greek conception of God, in particular the conception Greek philosophers had of God. Whereas Greek philosophers, it is said, conceived of God as a wise and good being, which in its wisdom and goodness could not but create the best possible world, the emphasis in Judaeo-Christian thought is not on God's wisdom and understanding but on God's will. The world is the way it is, not because God in his wisdom and understanding saw that, for it to be the best possible world, it had to be this way and hence because of his goodness had to create or arrange it in this way. Rather, the world is the way it is because God just wills it to be this way. In fact, it is often claimed that it is a merely contingent fact that there is a world in the first place. It is supposed to be a contingent fact, because God created it by a free act of will, when he could equally have chosen not to create a world. In contrast, it is claimed, the God of Greek philosophy, given his nature, cannot but create or arrange and order the world. Thus, it is claimed, for Greek philosophers the world's existence is a necessary fact.

The Christian view, following Genesis, is also that man is created in the image of God, and this is understood as crucially involving the idea that man has a free will in the image of God's will. Hence it is assumed that the human will, to be properly understood, has to be understood by analogy with the divine will. And this, I take it, is interpreted as somehow meaning that we too can do things by a sheer act of the will, perhaps even a sheer act of the will which defies explanation.

There is a lot to question about this way of thinking. I want at least to point out that we should not identify what some or many Christians think with what all Christians always have thought, let alone with Christianity, not to mention Judaism. I hardly have to note, furthermore, that generalizations about the Greek conception of God, or even just the God of Greek philosophers, are rather hazardous. But I want to begin by briefly remarking that we have already come across the idea in pagan philosophy that the human will is like the divine will. This is what Epictetus explicitly said, namely, that God has given us a will which is like his (see p. 77). I have also indicated that we shall understand the Stoic doctrine of the best possible world only if we see that the Stoic God does not create the world in light of some antecedent good he is trying to realize as well as he can, because he is attached to this good and has the wisdom to realize it as well as it can be realized. Rather, he himself is the paradigm of the good in his perfectly rational act of creation, and by his creation he defines what is to count as a so-called good and a so-called evil.

Far down into antiquity, to be sure, there is a contrast between how Plato, Aristotle, and other philosophers conceive of God and how Jews and Christians conceive of God. Already in the second century A.D. Galen notices this.[2] He does so while giving a teleological explanation of human eyelashes and their features. In the course of this account he comes to distinguish three kinds of explanation. There is (1) the kind of explanation atomists like Epicurus have to offer, according to which ultimately everything is the product of chance. But much better, Galen thinks, is (2) the kind of explanation Moses offers. For Moses at least takes into account that we cannot understand the way the world is unless we assume that there is an ultimate or first moving cause, which makes the world to be the way it is, namely, a demiurge or creator. Unfortunately, according to Galen, Moses also talks as if the way the world is were just a matter of God's will, as if God could will anything, absolutely anything, and it would be this way. Hence, Galen thinks, another view is yet superior, namely, the view (3) that the demiurge considers what *can* be done; for not everything can be done even by the demiurge; and so the demiurge will choose to do the best that can be done. Even the demiurge cannot provide human beings with eyelashes which stand up, as they should, if they are to fulfill their function, unless he also provides the eyelids with cartilaginous tissue in which the lashes can be firmly set. This, Galen says, is the view of Plato and the Greeks who followed the right method in the explanation of nature.

Dihle opens his book with a reference to this passage and some remarks on it which set the tone and direction for what follows.[3] Here, from the actual pen of an extremely learned pagan doctor and philosopher, we seem to have a contrast between an "intellectualistic" Greek way of looking at things and a "voluntaristic" Judaeo-Christian way of doing so, with the latter shaped by awe at an all-powerful God who is not constrained in any way in what he can do, and thus is not constrained in any way in what he can choose or will to do, and the realization of whose will cannot be thwarted or impeded by anything.

It is clear from Galen's reference to Plato and the demiurge that Galen was thinking of Plato's *Timaeus*. Galen himself was a Platonist, though he did not want to call himself or be called in this way. He had written several books on the *Timaeus*.[4] He was also very conservative. Hence he took the view that the demiurge of Plato's *Timaeus* is God. In this he was not in bad company.[5] But even by Galen's time there had been a good number of Platonists, for instance, Numenius, who denied this.[6] And, in part under the influence of Numenius, Plotinus was going to deny it, too. Soon afterwards every Platonist would follow suit.

The reason for this, to which I will turn shortly, is very simple and highly relevant for our purposes. But I want first to note that Galen, though a great physician and perhaps also a philosopher of some importance, was hardly a theologian or even someone with strong interests in theology. Perhaps, in fact, he showed good sense in thinking that the nature of the soul and the nature of God are things we can only speculate about, with *speculate (theōrein)* here having a pejorative sense. Apart from this, however, there is a problem in taking the demiurge of the *Timaeus* to be God, if we assume that God is the source and principle of everything there is. As described not only by Galen but also by Plato himself, the demiurge, in creating the world, looks up to the eternal paradigm consisting of the Forms and eternal truths that they define, and he acts in light of his conception of the

Good.[7] But, as we readers of Plato's *Republic* know, the Good is the source and principle also of the Forms and in this way of all that there is.[8] So the demiurge is at best two removes from God, the father of all. Hence, it is not surprising that the demiurge cannot do everything but is constrained in what he can do, not only by matter but also by antecedent reality, consisting of first the Good or God, and second the forms or eternal truths. Accordingly, Numenius, Plotinus, and all later Platonists distinguish God from the demiurge.

If we compare the God of Moses with the God of late ancient philosophers, we should take the God of Numenius or the God of Plotinus as our Greek object of comparison, rather than the God of Galen. Unfortunately, we know very little about Numenius. We do know, however, that he discussed Moses's conception of God in rather complimentary terms and that he had considerable influence on the theology of both Origen and Plotinus.[9] In the case of Plotinus's conception of God, we are in the good position of having his treatise "On Voluntariness and the Will of the One," where Plotinus gives up much of his usual reticence about the ultimate principle. Right at the outset (*Enn.* VI.8.1.5–6), he claims that God can do absolutely everything and that absolutely everything is up to him to do or not to do.[10]

Plotinus proposes that the whole of reality originates in an absolutely free and unconditioned act of divine will and that the free will of embodied human beings has to be understood as a faint image of this divine will. Needless to say, I do not have the ambition to establish the truth of Plotinus's view. What I hope to be able to do is simply to show that Plotinus has this view. From this we can infer that it is not quite right to hold that such a way of looking at the human will is specifically Judaeo-Christian or that because of it Christians were able to come to a conception or understanding of the will from which pagans were barred. In discussing Plotinus we shall also have a chance, which we have not had so far, to look in some detail at the way a Platonist received the originally Stoic notion of a free will.

PLOTINUS: "ON VOLUNTARINESS AND THE WILL OF THE ONE"

Plotinus begins his inquiry with the question of whether one can also ask, in the case of the gods, if there is anything which is up to them to do or not to do, which they are free to do or not to do, or whether this question arises only in the case of human beings, whose powerlessness is so manifest that one might well wonder whether there is anything which it is up to human beings to do or not to do and whether they have any freedom at all. In contrast, one might think that the gods have complete freedom and that therefore the question does not even arise in their case. Plotinus quickly answers this initial question by replacing the simple antithesis between gods and human beings with a more complex contrast between the One or God, the gods, and human beings. He also observes that there are considerable problems about the sense in which something can be said to be up to God or up to the gods. In the ensuing discussion it will turn out that this more complex contrast has to be refined into a contrast between the One or God, intellects (for the gods are intellects), rational souls, and human beings insofar as they are embodied.

In Plotinus's mind we are dealing here with a hierarchy of items which represent different levels of reality. There is the One or God or the Good, which is supposed to be the source and explanation of all reality. There is the intellect, which represents the level of immutable, eternal truths. There is the soul, which is meant to give concrete structure to physical reality in light of these abstract eternal truths. And there is the embodied human being, which is the product of such a structuring. For items at each of these four levels we want to know in what sense one can say that there is something which it is up to them to do or not to do.

In fact, Plotinus's treatise is concerned mainly with the freedom of God and the sense in which something can be said to be up to God to do or not to do. One can easily see why this would have to be his main concern. Plato sometimes, for instance, in the *Timaeus,* presents things as if the contents of the sensible world were best understood as the mirror image of an immaterial, purely intelligible, reality, albeit an image somewhat distorted by the inadequacies of the mirror. Correspondingly, Plotinus assumes that the characteristic features of items at a lower level of reality reflect the way the items at a higher level are represented, mirrored or imaged at a lower level. Thus what is an intellect at a higher level, unconcerned with the vagaries of the physical world and focused on eternal truth, will appear at a lower level in the image of a rational soul that is concerned with the vagaries of the physical world and the needs that life in it entails..

Indeed, just as you do not see two things when you look at a person and when you then look at the image of a person in a mirror but only one and the same thing, namely, the person, so the rational soul is nothing but the intellect as it appears at a lower level. Hence, if it is an important characteristic of embodied human beings that they are, or at least can be, free and it is part of their nature to be free or at least to be able to be free, this characteristic must have its source in a corresponding characteristic at the next higher level, a counterpart to human freedom at the level of the rational soul. This in turn must have its counterpart at the next higher level, the level of the pure disembodied intellect, and this in turn must have its source in some feature of the One or the Good. Hence what we are interested in is this feature of the One, which is the ultimate source of all freedom, including our freedom. It is only if we understand the One as the archetype of all freedom, to the extent that we can understand it, that we will understand our freedom for what it is, a reflection of a reflection of a reflection of divine freedom. It is because of this that in chapter 7, when he turns to discussing the freedom of the One, Plotinus can say that all other things receive from the One the powers or abilities which put them into a position in which one can say of them that they are free.

Nevertheless the freedom of the One cannot be the starting point of our inquiry. It is a dark and obscure matter for us. This is why it needs to be clarified. So we have to start from what is familiar to us—from the familiar fact that there is some sense in which there are things which it is up to us to do or not do. Our procedure here is typically Aristotelian. We start from things with which we are familiar; though they are not very clear, we at least have some intuitions about them. And, on their basis, we try to advance to the principles underlying them. They turn out to be very clear, once we have taken hold of them. With these principles in hand we return to look at the familiar things we started out from. Now, viewed in light of the principles we found, we also come really to understand the familiar things. Hence Plotinus's assumption must be that the sense and the way in which we are free ultimately become intelligible only in light of our understanding of divine freedom. And we have seen why in his view this must be so: our freedom is but a reflection or image of God's freedom.

More specifically, Plotinus does not just begin with something we are familiar with, namely, the presumed fact that we are free, but with the notion we have of something's being up to us, when we think that there are things which it is up to us to do or not to do. And we then work our way upwards. We look at the way and the sense in which individual human beings can be said to be free, at the way and the sense in which souls can be said to be free, and the way and the sense in which intellects can be said to be free. For we should not expect that the term *free* applies at all levels in the same sense and way. We are familiar from Aristotle with this idea of a hierarchy of senses. Aristotle starts out his career by thinking that there are lots of substances in the world, among them, Socrates and other human beings, plants, animals, stars, and God. Aristotle at this early point talks as if all these were substances in the same sense and way.[11] But later Aristotle made the first moves to correct this mistake. His own mature view seems to have been that God is a substance in a different sense and way from the sense and way in which corporeal beings are substances. Indeed, he seems to have assumed that the sense and way in which corporeal substances are substances has to be understood as a weakened version of the sense and way in which God is a substance, just as Aristotle also thinks that the way an artifact is a substance is a weakened version of the way a natural body is a substance. Plotinus thinks of freedom analogously. As we move up the hierarchy, we have to look for the appropriate sense and way in which things at this level can be said to be free, such that freedom at a lower level can be understood as a weakened analogue of freedom at the higher level. He calls this process of suitably changing the sense of "free" or "up to us" metaphor (*metapherein*, 1.19–20).

The notion of something's being up to us from which Plotinus

starts is this (1.31–33): something is up to us, if it is obedient *(dou-
leuei)* to our willing, and whether it comes about or does not is a
matter of the extent to which we will it. This, as it stands, is far
from transparent; indeed, there is a textual difficulty.[12] But the
context makes it very clear that for Plotinus something which
is up to us must satisfy two conditions: first, it must satisfy the
condition that, whether it comes about or does not come about,
is not already settled by the course of the world, independent
of us; and, second, whether it does comes about depends on us,
more specifically, on our willing to do it.

Something like the first condition is necessary because, as
Plotinus pointed out in the previous line (1.30), we may will to
do something, but the circumstances prevent us from doing it
and stand in the way of its getting done, though we want to do
it. Something which we are prevented from getting done, even
though we will to do it, maybe even strongly will to do it, is
surely not something which is up to us. So the first condition is
supposed to ensure that nothing in the world stands in the way
of our doing it.

To understand the second condition, we have to see, as becomes apparent from the immediately following lines, that Plotinus, like Alexander of Aphrodisias, is trying to distinguish between what is voluntary and what is up to us (see p. 95). Plotinus
characterizes the voluntary *(hekousion)* as what we do knowing
full well what we are doing and not being forced to do it. This
roughly corresponds, and obviously is meant to correspond, to
Aristotle's characterization of things for which we can be held
responsible *(hekontes)*. So, if you are mildly hungry and you see a
piece of food, you might have an appetite for this piece of food
which makes you get the piece of food and eat it. This is voluntary, because nothing forces you to eat the food, and you know

perfectly well what you are doing. But in requiring that an action, in order to be up to us, be due to a *willing*, Plotinus requires that such an action be motivated not by any kind of desire but by a desire of reason, as opposed to a nonrational desire, as in the example just considered.

This requirement seems plausible enough and, on the face of it, seems reasonably close to Alexander's conception of what is up to us and its difference from what is merely voluntary. But now Plotinus (in the immediately following lines 1.33–34) contrasts the voluntary and what is up to us by saying that the voluntary is that which we do knowingly and without being forced to do it, whereas something is up to us only if we are masters *(kyrioi)* over whether it gets done or not. This characterization will be the opening which allows Plotinus to drive a deep wedge between Alexander's and his own conception of what is to count as an action which is up to us, an action which is free. By the time Plotinus has finished with this operation, we shall have a notion of freedom which is remarkably close to the Stoic notion and in any case a great deal stronger and more demanding than Alexander's notion.

To see the force of this new characterization of what is up to us as being a matter of our being masters and of our being in charge of what we are doing, consider the following. Suppose you are the slave, the servant, or the subordinate of somebody who has authority or power over you. He is master *(kyrios)*, and he decides what gets done. It is his will which decides whether something gets done. So he orders you to do something. You do it. You do it voluntarily. He does not force you to do it, and you know what you are doing. But it is not the case that you do what you do, because you yourself decided or willed that this should get done. It was rather the will of your master that it should get done, indeed, that it should get done by you. Perhaps, left to your own devices, you would rather have done something else. Perhaps you do not even particularly like doing what you are told to do. In any case, it was not your will, your decision, or your idea that this should get done. Thus Plotinus is requiring, for an action to be up to us, that it be we ourselves who will to do it. There is a crucial shift of emphasis here from "Is this something you *will* to do, as opposed to something you merely desire to do?" to "Is this really what *you* will to do, as opposed to something somebody or something else wants you to do?" And Plotinus is going to exploit this shift in what follows.

In chapters 2 and 3 he argues that for your action to be up to you, it must be the case that your impulse, or your desire, to do it must be of a certain kind. It cannot be mere appetite *(epithymia)*. For an appetite has its origin in impressions which do not entirely depend on us, because they are produced by the body, in particular the bodily fluids.[13] Something analogous can be argued for the desire of spirit *(thymos)*. Thus, if we remember the three types of desire Plato and Aristotle distinguished, we are left with the desire of reason, or, as Plotinus now puts it, a consideration of reason *(logismos)*, combined with a desire. So we might think that Plotinus is now referring to the belief one has come to, that it would be a good thing to do something or other, and the desire of reason this belief gives rise to. Hence we might also think that we have now identified for Plotinus how an action must be motivated in order to count as free. But there is good reason why Plotinus prefers to talk about a rational consideration combined with desire. For it now turns out that it is not good enough for an action to count as free that it be an action which is motivated by a desire of reason. Plotinus insists that the desire in question should be a desire which has its source in your rational considerations, rather than the reverse. That is to say, the desire has to be generated by your rational considerations as to what would be a good thing to do. Only then will the desire be a willing, properly speaking.

The reverse case, I take it, is this. We have an appetite, and this generates a rational consideration to the effect that it would be a good thing to act accordingly. This rationalization in turn produces a willing. But this willing, given its origin in an appetite, will not suffice to qualify the action as free. Rather than being content with this restriction, Plotinus asks: What if your rational consideration led you to the wrong conclusion and hence the wrong desire, the wrong willing? According to him, the ensuing action is not free in this case either, because you do what you do only because you made a mistake and were misled by something or other. For the action to count as free, your conclusion must be the right conclusion and the desire the right desire to have. But even this is not good enough. For suppose it was just by chance that you happened on the right conclusion. As chance had it, you made two terrible logical howlers in your considerations, which cancelled each other out. So it is chance which made you do what you do. But we surely do not want the freedom of our actions to be a matter of chance. Plotinus then comes to the conclusion that the action is free only if it has its source in knowledge, that is, in the kind of insight and understanding which characterize the wise person. And thus we are back to Stoicism, almost. I say *almost* because, though Plotinus and the Stoics agree that only the wise person is free, there is considerable disagreement between them concerning the nature of this freedom.

The freedom which Plotinus allows to a human being in the flesh is highly qualified in two ways. One qualification has its origin in the fact that we have a nonrational part of the soul and a body. Hence we have certain desires by nature. We cannot help having them. As a result however much we may want to have something to eat, because we understand that it would be a good thing to eat and hence have the desire of reason to have something to eat, we also in eating are generally acting upon a natural nonrational desire and thus following the necessity of nature (2.13–15). Thus in eating, even if we are wise and virtuous, we are generally not entirely free. Our motivation is mixed. The second qualification on our freedom accrues to the embodied human being from the soul. So we should now turn to the soul and its freedom, to see what this qualification is.

As we may have imagined, the soul is free if it is wise and virtuous. Its function is to provide the embodied human being with a characteristically human life, ideally, a good life. Thus the soul also has to concern itself with the maintenance and welfare of the body. A wise Plotinian soul is not hostile to the body or to the visible world. Although divine providence in his view does not reach down into all the visible world's details, as the Stoics assume, its general order is providential, and it is part of this order that there be such a world with living beings in it, animated by souls. For any soul which can see, this visible world has its genuine, by no means meretricious, charms. After all, it is a reflection of eternal truths and the goodness and beauty of its source. The visible world is admittedly a faint reflection. And you have to keep in mind that you cannot expect bodies, including the body you yourself look after, to be any better than a body can be. What else can your body do, devoid of reason as it is, but clamor for the satisfaction of its needs?[14]

That the soul looks after the concerns of the body does not

mean, though, that it makes these concerns its own, becomes enamored with the body, or any body, and becomes attached to it or enslaved to it. It does not mean that the soul has to let itself be confused in such a way as to rationalize the desires of the body, as if the good of the body were its own good. The body's good consists in its being in a good functional state. The soul's good consists in its being wise and virtuous. Hence the soul's interest lies in attaining and maintaining its wisdom and virtue. And if acting wisely and virtuously involves giving up one's life, one's possessions, one's children, and even one's country, so be it (6.14–17).

This will suffice to explain the second qualification on our freedom. Even the soul's freedom is rather tenuous and qualified. Given the needs and desires of the body and all the more complex desires they draw in their train, the soul constantly becomes perturbed. It may come to be in a bad way, even if it is virtuous, and have to straighten itself out to maintain its virtue and freedom. Hence Plotinus's virtuous soul is not unchallenged in its freedom in the way the Stoic wise man is. Nor, it seems, does his virtuous person fit the image of Plato's or Aristotle's paragon, who has no source of motivation, no inclination left to act other than virtuously without any difficulty or conflict whatsoever. For Plotinus, it seems, the soul's union with the body inevitably presents a threat (5.27ff) to its virtue and hence its freedom.

There is yet another qualification on the freedom of the soul. Is it really free to choose to act in a virtuous way? Plotinus takes up this question in chapter 5, where we get an answer which is rather similar to the Stoics' and Origen's answer, though for different reasons. The Stoics and Origen went on the assumption that the way the world unfolds is determined by providence.

And this, in turn, required a qualification of the sense in which we are free to act in the world. This is not Plotinus's problem, since, as we have already noted, he does not believe that providence determines all that happens, including our actions. But he still has the problem that, even in his view of the world, it is not completely under our control whether we shall succeed in doing what we set out to do (5.4–5). So in this sense for him too it is not, strictly speaking, a matter of our choice whether something gets done by us which we will to do. We are not masters *(kyrioi)* over whether we succeed in doing what we set out to do (5.5): it is not *we* who decide whether something happens to get done. All we can do is our best (5.6–7). But then Plotinus has another worry. If we are virtuous, we will to act virtuously, even though it is not up to us whether we shall succeed in these actions. And now Plotinus questions whether we can really be said to will or want to do what is virtuous. Look at Hippocrates, he says (5.20). He is a wonderful doctor, and, needless to say, he will be glad to cure his patients of their afflictions. But surely, it is also the case that Hippocrates would prefer that his patients not be ill in the first place and that he not be put in a position where he has to cure somebody. In this sense his action is forced on him by the way the world is.

Consider virtuous action. If you are wise and virtuous, you will be courageous in war. But surely, it would be perverse to wish there to be a war so that you can be courageous. You would rather that there be no war in the first place and hence no need for your courage. You will be just in rendering justice. But surely, you would rather there be no need to render justice or to right wrongs. Seen in this light, even virtuous actions, for all the purity of their motivation, no longer seem to be really and unqualifiedly free. They are in some sense forced on you by the way the world is. If you do them nevertheless, it is because your soul, if it is wise and virtuous, is attached to the good, realizes that this is what needs to be done, and, on pain of becoming irrational, wills to do what needs to be done. But what it is really interested in is being rational, in having understanding and insight, and in its attachment to the good. This is what its good lies in, and it will beware of jeopardizing this good by letting itself become confused in such a way as to make you act nonvirtuously.

Plotinus infers from this that the freedom of the soul is not primarily a freedom to make us do things in the world but is rather an internal freedom to think the right thoughts and form the right desires, based on an insight into reality and an unconfused understanding of the good. This state of the soul Plotinus calls a second intellect *(nous tis allos)*, and he says of the soul in this state that it has been "intellectualized," as it were *(noōthēnai; 5.34–36)*. In this state the soul does not allow us to be slaves.

With this we can now turn to the intellect. We have to understand that Plotinus's intellects, unlike Origen's, are not created. They are eternal. They know the eternal truths. They have as good and firm an understanding of the good as a perfect intellect can have. They eternally contemplate the truth. They understand that their good consists precisely in their contemplating the truth. So this is what they want to do. This is what they immensely enjoy doing. And they enjoy it all the more, since they invariably succeed in what they are doing. They are perfectly free. They can do whatever they want to do, given that this is all they ever want to do. It is also guaranteed that their being able to do whatever they want to do does not lead to any undesirable consequences. All they ever want to do, inasmuch as they are disembodied intellects, is to know and understand the truth and its source in goodness. There is nothing to distract them from this, nothing to make them want to do anything else, nothing to prevent them from doing what they want to do.

We must find this a rather curious form of freedom, given our modern notions. The intellects, quite literally, can do nothing except what they are doing; they cannot choose to do anything else. If we remember Alexander's notion of freedom as involving the ability to choose otherwise, many ancients must already have seen a difficulty here. Plotinus addresses this difficulty in various ways. He says (4.4ff) that one might worry whether the intellect is free. For, though it is up to the intellect to do what it does, it is not up to it not to do what it does. And one might argue (4.23ff) that the intellect, given its nature, cannot but do what it does. Against this Plotinus argues that the intellect and the nature of the intellect are not two different things, such that the nature of the intellect decides or determines what the intellect has to do and the intellect then does it. For Plotinus (in this, following Aristotle), the nature or essence of immaterial objects is identical to the objects themselves. So the intellect cannot be said to be forced by its nature to do what it does since the intellect *is* its own nature. But tellingly, the main drift of Plotinus's argument is to invert things against our modern expectations. The intellect is unqualifiedly free precisely because there is no chance whatsoever that it might act otherwise, that it might choose otherwise, that it might even be tempted to choose otherwise. To think differently, Plotinus claims (4.20–23), is to think that what is bad about slavery is that one is not free to do evil things or to do things which it is not in one's interest to do. What is bad about slavery, rather, is that one does not have the ability *(exousia)* to pursue one's own good. Instead the slave is supposed to pursue the good of somebody else. But the intellects are free to do precisely those things which it is in their interest to do, which they ardently want to do, and which they enjoy doing. They are not forced by anything or anybody else to do this. So what is unfree about them?

In contrast, this freedom of the intellect shows the tenuousness of the soul's freedom in that, even if the soul is virtuous, it is constantly tempted by the body to act otherwise, might choose to act otherwise, and could act otherwise. The limitations of human freedom are evident in the fact that we or the soul, so long as we are not virtuous, constantly do act otherwise, even if we strive to attain our good, namely, virtue and wisdom. Alexander had located freedom and merit primarily in this state of not yet being fully virtuous but striving to be virtuous (p. 100). But, Plotinus argues, striving for a good which one does not yet have or which one is lacking is just another sign of lacking freedom and not being self-determined. For, in this case, one is driven by something outside oneself. Freedom, for Plotinus, would rather seem to be a matter of the secure possession and control over what one wills and wants. In any case, we see sufficiently by now why he thinks that an intellect is unqualifiedly free, but a soul is free only insofar as it has become like an intellect with its freedom qua soul something highly tenuous and qualified.[15] Finally, we see that the embodied human being is free, insofar as its soul is free, but that its freedom to do things in the world is so highly qualified that *freedom* hardly seems the right word for it.

With this, then, we can at last turn to God. It is often said that Jews and Christians were monotheists, whereas pagans were polytheists. I am inclined to think that almost all philosophers in late antiquity were monotheists.[16] They distinguished between *ho theos* (God or the God) and the gods—beings superior to humans, which, because of their goodness, enjoy eternal bliss or, in the case of Stoicism, enjoy bliss until the next world conflagration. If you do not like the word *gods*, Porphyry tells us to call them *angels*.[17] Plotinus at the outset of the treatise very clearly makes the same distinction (compare 1.4 with 1.6 and with 1.18–19). The gods are the intellects. They do indeed enjoy a life of eternal bliss, but they would never dream of thinking of themselves as God. It is sometimes said that, even if Greek philosophers did believe in one thing which they called "God," this was an abstract principle, rather than a personal God. Now it is perfectly true that the God of Plotinus and Platonists like him is an exceedingly abstract principle. Yet *abstract* does not seem to be quite the right word, because it still suggests that God is something or other which one can abstract. The right word, rather, is *transcendent*. Still, it is easy to see why one might get the impression that their God is not a personal God. The Platonists do refer to this transcendent principle of all there is, but as a rule they steadfastly refuse to say anything about it. And the reason for this is simple and should be easily understood by any Christian, especially by those devoted to the spiritual life. There quite literally cannot possibly be anything which it would be true to say about God. For God is the source and origin of all truth and existed before all truth. So the appropriate attitude is one of silence. Thus in our treatise (II.1–2) Plotinus, having raised the question of what this principle is, asks, "Or shall we, having fallen silent, just leave?"

Ennead. VI.8 is the only treatise where Plotinus breaks this silence systematically and at great length. All of a sudden we are confronted with a God nobody could possibly deny personhood to, except, of course, that it is not true to say, either, that God is a person. Why does Plotinus break this silence? One reason is that Platonism suffers from a deep structural difficulty, which I alluded to earlier. Everything is supposed to be understood in terms of one ultimate principle, but this principle, being ultimate, is itself beyond intellectual understanding and beyond truth. But, if we want to understand freedom, we have to understand how the freedom of the intellect, and subsequently all other freedom, has its source in this first principle. So we have to resort to language, knowing full well that we are misusing language. The problem is not that there is anything inadequate about our language or that these objects for which we use this language are too elevated for our pedestrian discourse, which we developed, after all, to talk about more mundane things. The problem is that no language in principle, however ideal it is by whatever standards, will be applicable.

This, of course, does not exclude the possibility of our saying that one should not say anything about God, and this is literally true. Nor does it exclude the possibility of our saying that one can say that there are certain things in particular which it would be quite misleading to say about God. We can, for instance, say that it would be blasphemous to say that the world consisted of so many trees, so many tigers, so many human beings, et cetera, et cetera, and one God. Plotinus at the very outset of his discussion of God's freedom, in 7.11ff, refers to just such a terrible thing to say *(ho tolmēros logos)*, as he calls it. The terrible thing to say is that God just happens to be the way he is, and, given that he is this way, he cannot help but act the way he does; put differently, he is forced to act the way he does by the way he is, and the way he is, he just happens to be like.

It is easy to see why Plotinus, and indeed any Greek philosopher from Plato and Aristotle onwards, would find this a monstrous thing to say. The search for ultimate principles is the search for principles in terms of which everything can be understood and explained but which do not themselves require any further explanation. But what we get in "the terrible thing to say" is the assumption that how the world is has its source in a brute fact which does admit of an explanation, to the extent that we can say that it is by chance that God is this way and hence the world is this way: we could have had a different God, and the world could have been otherwise. This view, which is evidently so abhorrent to Plotinus, shares at least one feature with the view Christians often attribute to him and Platonists like him, namely, the view that God does what he does of necessity, because it is his nature so to act. This is supposed to stand in stark contrast to the Christian view that God created the world by a free act of the will, as a result of which the world is contingent, though God himself is a necessary being.

Here we find Plotinus vehemently rejecting the view that God is not free because he had no say in what he is like or because it was not up to him to be like this, and because, being a thing like this, he is forced to act the way he does. Perhaps we get clearer about the nature of the monstrous claim if we take into account that it is the more specific claim that it just *happens* to be the nature of God to be good and so he cannot but act well.[18] But God (so the claim continues) had no hand in his being good, since it was not up to God to be good by doing what it takes to become virtuous or wise; if this were so, we might also say that his actions, once he was good, were free, rather than necessitated or forced, because they at least were based on earlier free choices, as God was trying to become good. But God is not like this. His very nature is to be good. And so there is nothing free about his good actions or about his creation.

Plotinus continues for many chapters to demolish this terrible claim, for instance, by arguing that at God's level there exists no chance, because chance already presupposes a certain kind of plurality and regularity, against the background of which something can be said to be, or to happen, by chance, which we find only at the level of the world we live in. He also argues that there can be no necessity at God's level, because necessity appears for the first time at the lower level of necessary truths. What we are here interested in, though, is what Plotinus has to say in the end.

I noted earlier that in the case of the intellects Plotinus is heavily relying on Aristotle. According to Aristotle, in the case of individual human beings we can distinguish between (1) the human being as such; (2) the intellect, which is the ability or potentiality to think, which we may, or may not, exercise; and (3) an exercising of this ability in an actual thought. A crucial part of Aristotle's theory is that the intellect, being the mere possibility that one may think, exists only actually as an actual thought.[19] When we now come to the eternal, disembodied, and immaterial intellects of Plotinus, there is no longer anything which *has* an intellect as distinct from actually being an intellect. And since there is nothing here which has this intellect, there is also nothing which could exercise or fail to exercise this ability. These intellects eternally think. And since the intellect exists only as a thought, these intellects are just thoughts. What is more, since they are immaterial, they are identical to their nature or essence. So in the case of these intellects, the intellect as such, the nature of the intellect, and the activity of the intellect all coincide in one thing, namely, a thought. Nevertheless we can still make formal distinctions. We can still say that the intellect thinks the way it does because it lies in the nature of the intellect to think in this way. On the other hand, we can deny that its nature forces the intellect to think in this way and that therefore the intellect is not free because the nature of the intellect is not one thing which could decide, the way a slave master could, what the intellect has to do.

If we now turn to God, because of God's absolute simplicity, even this formal distinction is gone. It is not that in the case of God we could still, at least formally or conceptually, distinguish between God, his nature, and his activity. Hence it does not make any sense to say that God is forced by his nature to do what he does. This did not even make sense at the level of the intellect. Hence, a fortiori, it does not make any sense in the case of God. What is more, it does not make any sense to say that God just happens to have this nature. For that would presuppose our being able to distinguish between God and the nature he happens to have. But, we may ask, how does this shed any light on God's freedom and, more important in a way, on freedom in general? We have argued that it cannot be ultimately by chance that God does what he does, by happening to be the sort of thing he is, and by acting as this sort of thing naturally does. In any case, we certainly do not want to say that it is by chance that God does this rather than that. We have also argued that it is not by necessity that God acts the way he does. There is nothing which could force him to act the way he does. We certainly cannot say that his nature forces him to do so. What other possibility is left, then, but to say, if one is to say anything, that God acts the way he does because he himself wills to act this way?

Now, this, though not literally true, is enlightening in the following way. For now we see what the essence of freedom is— the ability to do something because one wills or wants to do it oneself, rather than because something or somebody else makes one do it or even makes one want to do it. And we also see how this freedom at different levels would take different forms and become diminished. For, once we turn to the intellects, there is at least a formal distinction between them and their nature. And so we can say that it is their nature which makes them do what they do, namely, contemplate the truth. But they are by nature good. They have a nature such that they cannot do anything else but what an intellect is meant to do, namely, contemplate the truth. Nevertheless they are free, because they do what they do, because they themselves will to do it, and nobody or nothing else forces them to do it. Indeed, they are secure in their freedom to do what they want to do.

When we turn to souls, the matter is different. For it is not the nature of the soul to be good, to be wise and virtuous. It has to acquire a state of wisdom and virtue out of which it does things, because it wills to do them. And this state is not secure. This is why it can choose otherwise and act otherwise. This is not indicative of a higher degree of freedom but rather of a diminished freedom. In the case of the embodied human being, not only does its soul have this diminished freedom at best, its body does not even have any freedom. It is bound by natural necessity. Hence, for instance, a human being cannot do whatever it wants to do, unlike intellects.

Let us return to God's will. We should not categorically say that God is free or that God wills anything. For neither expression is strictly true. We use them to fend off a misunderstanding of God and, at the same time, to keep our minds open to the idea that God is the source of our freedom. But, if we say this at all, we also have to remember that in God, given his absolute simplicity, there is no distinction between God's nature and God's activity. So, if we say that God does what he does because he wills to do it, we might also say that God is the way he is because he wills or wants to be this way. And this makes some sense. For, after all, Plotinus insists that God is beautiful *(kalos)* and lovable *(erasimos)*, indeed that he is love and love of himself (15.1–2). So, of course, he would want to be the way he is. But we should also note that there is no distinction between this willing and what God wills. That distinction has a place only at the lower levels, most conspicuously at the level of the soul and of embodied human beings, where willing and being a certain way or doing something might be entirely separated. We might will to do something but be unable to do it. We might wish to be a certain way but be unable to be like this.[20]

Hence, if we do speak of God's willing at all, what we have here is an act of the divine will with which the whole of reality, from the intellects downwards, begins. And it is not a forced act of the will but a free act of the will. Therefore it cannot be true that the world's dependence on God's will is a specifically Judaeo-Christian idea. It also cannot be true that, according to Plotinus, and the Platonists like him, the existence of the world and its general character are a necessary consequence of God's nature. I have to add at this point that Plotinus's view on this question comes as a great surprise for anybody whose understanding of Greek philosophy is formed by the study of Plato and Aristotle. But we have to remember that Plotinus was writing this treatise about 590 years after Aristotle's death.

Nevertheless one eminent Plotinian scholar, A. H. Armstrong, tried to persuade us that Plotinus was writing under Christian influence.[21] Armstrong starts out by claiming that the question of God's freedom did not seriously occupy philosophers until roughly the time of Plotinus and that, when it came to occupy them, it was "probably due to Jewish and Christian contacts" (399). And he goes on to suggest that "the monstrous claim" had its source actually in an objection made against Plotinus by a

Christian acquaintance who claimed that, according to Plotinus, the creation is a necessary consequence of God's nature. This objection is supposed to have made Plotinus rethink his position.

I find this incredible. One reason is that Plotinus's God had all along been a level above any necessity. So there can never have been any need for Plotinus to take this criticism seriously. Armstrong himself later acknowledges that his suggestion has not generally been accepted.[22] I dwell on this point because it is becoming increasingly clear that there is very little to the so-called Judaeo-Christian way of thinking about things which is specifically Judaeo-Christian. What primarily springs to mind is the Pharisaean-Christian doctrine of the resurrection of the body. Not surprisingly, given that Christianity is a historical phenomenon, there are pagan parallels for almost everything else. Hence we should resist the temptation to think that striking similarities, as we slowly become aware of them, either are not similarities at all or are due to Christian influence.

In any case, we have seen that there are deep-rooted reasons in Plotinus's philosophy which make him say that God has a will which is free. Moreover we also find in Plotinus the view that our will and our freedom are in the image of God's will and God's freedom. It is a crucial part of the point of the whole treatise to show this.

Finally, it seems to me that Plotinus does not make the mistake which some Christians seem to be so eager to make. God's will, by definition, is absolute and unconditioned. Anthropomorphically speaking, there is nothing which God could orient himself by in willing what he does will. But now the Christian idea seems to have arisen that our will is in the image of God precisely in that we are free to make absolute and unconditioned choices which have no further explanation. This surely is a terrible mistake. Our freedom must consist in the freedom to make the choices which are appropriate in the light of what the world is like by God's will. Our choices are, or rather should be, conditioned by the reality God created. That God's will is unconditioned is just due to the fact that there is no reality antecedent to God which could condition or even determine his choice.

This is one more reason why we should keep in mind that it is not strictly speaking true that God has a free will. But, setting this aside, we are not God. There is a reality into which we are born, which we have to deal with, and in the light of our understanding of which we have to make our choices. To think that we can just will something by a sheer act of volition is rather close to deluding oneself into thinking that one is God.

CHAPTER NINE

Augustine: A Radically New Notion of a Free Will?

A generation or two ago Augustine appeared in a very different light from what he would, or should, appear in nowadays. If fifty or even thirty years ago one knew something about ancient philosophy, one had for the most part studied the pre-Socratics, Plato, and Aristotle and had enjoyed reading authors like Lucretius, Cicero, and Plutarch. If one then went further down the canonical list of outstanding philosophers living after Aristotle and turned, as one likely would, to Augustine, one could not fail to be struck by his radical difference of outlook in almost every detail. It was tempting to assume that this radical difference had a great deal, if not everything, to do with Augustine's Christianity. So it is not surprising that accounts of medieval philosophy often begin with Augustine, as if, being a Christian, he were almost already a medieval figure.

In fact, Augustine is very much an ancient figure. The difference in outlook between Plato and Aristotle, on the one hand, and Augustine, on the other hand, is not, in the first place, a matter of Augustine's Christianity but of his being a late ancient figure. This is true even of Augustine's religious outlook, for even Christianity itself is very much a phenomenon of late antiquity. It was, of course, well known that Augustine was heavily indebted to the kind of Platonism we find in Plotinus and in Porphyry. This is obvious from his own remarks, for instance, in the *Confessions* VIII.2. But a few decades ago very little was understood about this Platonism and about the views of Plotinus and Porphyry. The extent of Augustine's indebtedness to this Platonism, whether direct or indirect, remained unclear.

Today things have changed, or at least they should have changed. We are now beginning to have a much better understanding of the Platonism Augustine was so indebted to. We also have a much better understanding of Stoicism, though the extent of Stoicism's pervasive influence on Augustine is still insufficiently appreciated. Nor is it fully clear through what channels this Stoicism reached Augustine. In large part, of course, it came through Cicero, who, though he was an Academic skeptic, had espoused the kind of Philonean skepticism which allowed for the qualified adoption of philosophical views; these, for the most part, turned out to be Stoic or inspired by Stoicism.[1]

In Augustine's time the study of Cicero was perhaps the most crucial part of any higher education for Westerners, especially for a professional rhetorician, as Augustine was in his early career. But we also have to remember in this context that by his time Platonism had absorbed large doses of Stoicism. The ultimate dividing line between the two schools was the Platonist belief in a transcendent God and an immaterial realm of reality, as opposed in Stoicism to a purely material reality with God immanent therein. Below this dividing line a Platonist could afford to borrow almost anything from Stoicism. Thus Porphyry (*VP* 17) talks of a philosopher, Trypho, whom he calls a Stoic and Platonist. Much of the Stoic influence on Augustine will have been mediated by Platonist sources. Finally, it seems that Ambrose, in whose circle in Milan Augustine became familiar with Platonism, was himself heavily indebted to Stoicism, especially Stoic ethics.[2]

Beyond Augustine's heavy indebtedness to Platonism and Stoicism, we need to remember that he was joining a tradition, more than two centuries old, of systematizing Christian belief. While this was heavily indebted to Platonism and Stoicism, it was also now developing its own momentum. Here it is important to remember that Augustine studied Marius Victorinus, following the advice of Simplicianus, a Platonizing priest who had baptized Ambrose and who was himself to become bishop of Milan.[3] Victorinus had been a highly successful rhetorician who late in life had converted to Christianity. He had translated logical writings of Aristotle and also, it seems, some treatises of Plotinus's and Porphyry's, presumably the *Platonici libri* which had such an impact on Augustine.[4] He also wrote books on the Trinity, and exegetical works, remarkably all of them on Paul's *Epistles*. Augustine became eager to follow in his footsteps (see *Conf.* VIII.5.10).

What is true of Augustine's thought in general is true in particular about his thought on the will. His view of the will is pervasively Stoic but embedded in a Platonist notion of the world. It is also responsive to a now quite substantial Christian tradition of thought on the matter and, not least in my opinion, to Victorinus. Hence we should from the outset be highly suspicious of any claim that Augustine initiated a radically new notion of the will that was inspired by a Judaeo-Christian tradition of thinking about God and the world. After all, we should not forget that ever since Justin Martyr's days, or at least since the time of Origen, there had been a good deal of Christian thought on the matter, and that, for Origen, given his life first in Alexandria and especially later in Caesarea, Judaism was a very powerful living reality, in which he took an active interest and for which he had a level of respect such as, I suspect, is rather missing in Augustine. In any case, it should strike us as curious that many generations of rather eminent Christian authors should have missed out on a distinctive feature of Judaeo-Christian thought concerning a matter to which they attributed such great importance. It seems more promising instead to expect Augustine, given his originality, to have something new to say on the will but new on a much more modest scale and within the confines of an evolving Christian position. We have already considered Origen's view. Not surprisingly, given the tradition Augustine is working in, there are striking similarities between his and Origen's positions. But there are also noteworthy differences. Hence it seems to me to be most promising to focus on these similarities and differences and to see where the differences come from.

I will argue for the conclusion that, to a large extent, the differences are due to the fact that Augustine follows the Stoic view on freedom much more closely than Origen does. But I want to anticipate this proposal by addressing immediately what I take to be the main argument for the claim that Augustine's notion of the will is radically different from anything we find in Greek philosophy.

The argument is this. In Greek philosophy, it is claimed, intention or willing appears either before or after cognition as its result or by-product. We readily see what is meant. I argued in the second of these chapters that Plato and Aristotle do not have a notion of a will, since for them a willing, a desire of reason, is a direct result of one's cognitive state: once one sees something to be good, one wills it. And, of course, it is also true that, according to Plato, Aristotle, and the Stoics, one naturally wills or wants to have cognition or knowledge. So our life seems to turn around, and depend on, our cognitive state.

Augustine's alleged difference from this position is that he, supposedly, separates willing from cognition: rather than willing's being made a direct function of cognition, it is itself made to be a crucial factor involved in cognition. Augustine's will is even involved in every act of perception. Dihle explicitly contrasts Stoic and Platonic psychology with Augustine's "new" psychology. For them "the element of will occurs before and after the very act of intellectual perception. . . . In the view of St. Augustine, will indeed partakes in the very act of cognition and is by no means restricted to preliminary and subsequent activities."[5] Dihle also points out, quite rightly, the strong connection Augustine sees between the will and faith and how Augustine again and again insists that you first have to believe on faith, before you can understand (p. 129). Now this certainly is not a notion of a will we find in Plato or Aristotle or one that we find in Peripatetics or in most Platonists. But, in fact, it is precisely a version of the more complex notion of the will which we found in Epictetus, a notion which Origen was already deploying, except that Augustine exploits its possibilities much more fully than Origen ever did.

Let us briefly recall the distinction we made between a less complex version of the notion of a will and the fuller and more complex version we actually find in Epictetus. In the less complex version, which was the one for the most part adopted by Peripatetics and Platonists, our will is responsible for only some of our choices and decisions, namely, those that constitute willings, one's willing to do something. But in the more complex notion, the will is responsible for all of our choices and all of our decisions concerning our impressions. Thus the will is also responsible for our choice to give assent to an ordinary, nonimpulsive impression, like the impression that $2 + 2 = 4$. Such an assent does not constitute a willing but a believing. This distinction between the kinds of choices for which the will is responsible is crucial also in the following regard. As we saw, it is important for this doctrine of the will that, properly speaking, you cannot choose to cross the street but only will to cross the street, since in principle it is not entirely under your control whether you manage to get across the street. In contrast, you can choose to give assent to an ordinary nonimpulsive impression, and thus you can choose to believe something, since in principle it is entirely under your control whether you give assent or not to an impression. So you can choose to believe something, but you cannot will to believe something, because to will is to will to do something. This last distinction, though, gets lost in Augustine, because Augustine renders both *willing* and *choosing* by *velle*.

Now, given what we have just said, it should be obvious that for a late Stoic like Epictetus the will is crucially involved in every act of cognition. It is, after all, standard Stoic doctrine that even perception *(aisthēsis)* involves an act of assent to a perceptual impression. What holds for perceptions holds true for all cognitions *(katalēpseis)*, which are constituted by an act of assent to a cognitive impression *(phantasia katalēptikē)*,[6] and indeed for all beliefs, whether perceptual or not, whether cognitive or not, whether true or false. They all involve assent, and hence they involve both a choice to give assent and a will disposed to choose to give assent.

For this reason the Stoics also have no difficulty with the idea that one chooses to believe something, even without knowing it to be the case or without understanding why it is the case. They believe in oracles and in divination. So they think that you ought to choose to believe what the god tells you, even if you have no independent means of verifying its truth, let alone are able to understand why things are the way the god tells you. Thus the Stoic notion of the will leaves ample room for the idea that one chooses to believe something on trust or on faith. Hence also in this regard Augustine's notion of the will as something which is centrally involved in any cognitive act is nothing new. It is just the Stoic notion of the will. And, incidentally, this Stoic notion is also supposed to account for whether you can hold on to your beliefs or are easily talked out of them and whether you too quickly and easily espouse beliefs which you are then not able to hold on to.

Having clarified the fact that Augustine's notion of the will is just a version of the more complex Stoic notion of the will, let us now, more systematically, consider his doctrine of freedom and a free will. We get his most detailed and systematic exposition in the early treatise *De libero arbitrio voluntatis,* which was written in two stages between 388 and 395.[7] This is also, in a sense, the authoritative exposition of his view. When Augustine, at the end of his life, reviews his writings in the so-called *Retractationes,* he talks in some detail about the *De libero arbitrio* and insists that it still fully represents his view, even though in certain places he would now choose a different formulation. In the *Retractationes* (2) we also learn, as we may already have gathered from the *De libero arbitrio* itself (I.10), that the treatise is directed against the Manichaeans, who attribute the origin of evil to God, the Creator, in having created us in such a way that, because of having a body-dependent soul, we cannot but do evil.[8]

It is quite striking how much of Augustine's literary output is polemical in nature, directed against schismatics or heretics. A heresy which was going to preoccupy him increasingly for almost the last twenty years of his life was Pelagianism. It is a matter of great scholarly controversy what Pelagius actually had taught.[9] Augustine, like most late ancient authors, was not particularly eager to do justice to his opponents. In the *Retractationes* he characterizes the Manichaeans as if they believed in an evil creator of the Gnostic kind. In fact the Manichaean creator is good, though not all powerful; he is confronted with a force of darkness, and by his creation he is trying to liberate what is light and good in us. In the same vein Augustine also presents the Pelagians as if they believed that our will is so free that there is no room for divine grace (*Retr.* 3). It seems obvious that in fact Pelagius simply emphasized the ability of human beings to attain the good life, to do something of merit which would earn them a good life, without denying the need for divine grace altogether. So the issue is, rather, whether the Pelagians left more room for the contribution human beings can, and need to, make to their attainment of the good life than Augustine was willing to allow for, given his insistence on the pervasive need for grace.

One might think that this controversy would lead to a further evolution of Augustine's doctrine of a free will. But in the *Retractationes* (3–6) he explains in detail that the *De libero arbitrio* already, at least implicitly, if not explicitly, contains his answer to Pelagianism. Hence, in his view of the matter, there was no need to change his position on the free will. What there was need for was a systematic doctrine of grace and its relation to freedom. It has to be said, though, that the *De libero arbitrio* does not give one as clear a view as one would like of what, according to Augustine, the role of grace is. Part of the reason for this presumably is that Augustine at this early point had not yet fully thought through these matters.

We may best understand Augustine's thought about freedom and a free will in this work if we view it largely as a response to Manichaeism, in a way analogous to our taking Origen's doctrine of a free will to be a response to Gnosticism and astral determinism.[10] Their point of departure was the undeniable fact that we are born with a natural endowment or constitution and in circumstances which seem to make it impossible for most, if not all of us, to live a good life. Both Origen and Augustine found themselves confronted with doctrines which explained this state of affairs by making a creator, or ruler or rulers, of this world ultimately responsible for our misdeeds. They both had to reject this view as incompatible with the Creator's goodness. They did so, relying on a doctrine of freedom and free will, by attributing to human beings themselves the difficulties they find themselves in as a result of their own choice and doing. But they disagreed on the particular way in which they analyzed the situation in which we find ourselves, how we got into it, and how we may get out of it. Even here, in this analysis, there remains a striking amount of agreement.

Let us begin with the situation in which we find ourselves. Augustine's picture of it is a great deal gloomier than Origen's. For Origen the situation is that we find it very, very difficult to resist sin, so difficult as to lend plausibility to the view that perhaps many of us are in principle unable not to sin and in principle unable to attain the good life. For Augustine the picture is that the world is full of evil, not just full of wrongdoing, but also full of suffering wrong. And not just this. Catastrophes overcome us in the form of floods, droughts, pests, wars, famines, and personal disasters. They seem to hit innocent and guilty alike. In any case, there is no apparent connection between what somebody did and the evil that befalls him. This is most obvious in the case of infants. For more than the next hundred years particular attention will be given to the fate of newly born children who, surely, had done nothing to deserve the misery and the suffering to which they often were exposed. It is this evil we are born into whose source and origins the *De libero arbitrio* formally sets out to identify. And in I.77 Augustine describes lovingly how we all in this life are constantly torn apart and driven by fears and desires which make our life miserable. It is difficult, indeed, to see how in this state one could live a good and well-satisfied life.

We are not surprised to hear that Augustine thinks, like Origen, that it is not God who is to blame for this but that we have brought it on ourselves by our own doing, by our choice, by our own free choice. This is how the doctrine of freedom and a free will comes in. But there are two differences. We noted that in Origen the intellects went wrong through carelessness. But these seemed to be minor missteps, as it were, which could be rectified and which only in their accumulation would lead to grave consequences. And even these consequences, though grave indeed, in the case of human souls were not painted in such relentlessly gloomy and depressing colors as in Augustine. So Augustine prepares himself and us to expect that we must have done something terrible indeed to deserve as miserable a life as this. And there is another difference. In Origen it is perfectly clear in what sense we all, each and every one of us, are responsible for the situation we are in. All of us who live in this physical world are intellects who fell. However, we did not fall badly enough to become downright vicious but only enough to deserve this remedial punishment. In Augustine it is not so clear who did what, as a result of which we all suffer this punishment.

The reason for this is the notorious difficulty Augustine had with the question of the origin of the soul, which, it seems, he felt unable to resolve fully to his satisfaction for the rest of his life. He considered four possibilities.[11] First, the rational soul preexists our earthly existence but falls through sin and ends up as a soul attached to a body. Second, the rational soul preexists, it is sent to take care of a body, but in the course of its mission becomes culpable. Third, each soul is created ad hoc by God to ensoul the body generated through sexual procreation by the parents. Fourth, the soul itself is transmitted by sexual procreation. This last view, called traducianism, though not uncommon, was quite unsatisfactory, since it basically involved the assumption that the soul is a function of the body; that might account for a nonrational soul but not for a rational soul, at least given a Platonist's, and Augustine's, dualistic view of the latter.

It has been argued, rather pervasively, by O'Connell, that the first view was the position Augustine favored at least when he wrote the *De libero arbitrio*.[12] This is a view which Plotinus had entertained as a possibility (*Enn.* IV.8.4). And it is Origen's view, if we disregard the fine difference between intellects and rational souls. But Augustine did not firmly commit himself to this view even in the *De libero arbitrio* or later. In fact, in some places he clearly seems to reject the assumption of preexisting souls. But as soon as we reject the first two options, we are faced with the difficulty that it cannot be literally true that each of us individually brought it upon himself to be born into this world of misery. For if we did not exist before our birth even as rational souls, how could we have done sufficient wrong to deserve being born into this misery? In this case, the terrible deed which got us into the position we are in cannot be something we individually did. It must, then, be something like the original sin of Adam. But this raises the question of why we should be held responsible and suffer for something done by Adam.

There are answers to this, both in the East and in the West. They involve the development of appropriate metaphysical theories with very different conceptions of individuals and kinds from the ones we are used to. It was theories of this sort which later in the West give rise to the realism-nominalism debate.[13] In brief the idea is this. Man or mankind is a real thing, of which we are parts in the way something is part of a collective, say, a soldier part of an army. We assume that God did not create a particular man, Adam, but Man or mankind, just as God did not become a man, but Man or mankind. But mankind exists only as a collection of parts like Adam or Jesus. So, when God created Man, he created such a collection or collective. And it was this collective, mankind as a whole, which sinned when Adam sinned. Hence it is mankind as a whole which is responsible for this sin. Needless to say, such a theory would need a great deal of work.

But, whatever the difficulties involved, Augustine became increasingly inclined to believe that the terrible deed for which we are held responsible was not something which we individually actually had done. Presumably, he did so under the influence of Paul's *Letter to the Romans*, 5:12ff, according to which sin came into the world through one human being.

There is another wavering on Augustine's part in the *De libero arbitrio*. Throughout the treatise he is inclined to think that this terrible deed, whether we are responsible for it individually or collectively, was done by a rational being who was wise and virtuous. It is easy to see why he would be inclined to think so. If

God had created us in a state of ignorance and lack of virtue, it would not be surprising if we got confused and made a mistake. But then, for this very reason, it would also be difficult to understand why God did not create us with a basic understanding of the world and of the good. Moreover, if we were created in a state of ignorance and lacking virtue, it would be difficult to see what was so terrible about this terrible deed. What else could God expect? What would make it such a terrible deed would be precisely this, that human beings had the wisdom and the virtue that were needed not to go wrong (see I.79–81). So this again sounds very much like Origen with his assumption of visible intellects which were created wise and virtuous to a sufficient degree not to fall. But in this very context where (I.81) Augustine suggests that perhaps our present situation is due to the fact that, as preexisting rational souls, we deserted the safe stronghold of virtue *(arx virtutis)* to submit ourselves to the slavery of appetite by our own choice—in this very context Augustine makes a move which opens up, or rather indicates, a wide rift between himself and Origen.

He relies here on the Stoic division of mankind into the wise and virtuous and free, on the one side, and the foolish and vicious and unfree, on the other side. We *were* wise and virtuous and free, and now we are foolish and vicious and enslaved. But this cannot be quite right. For, although, according to the Stoics, we indeed are now foolish, vicious, and enslaved, we never were actually wise, virtuous, and free. Moreover, according to the standard Stoic theory, once, by liberating yourself, you are wise, virtuous, and free, you will never of your own will give up this freedom. For this reason I argued that the wisdom and the virtue Origen attributed to his intellects was in principle a wisdom and virtue which, though it admitted of further improvement, was never entirely perfect. This is why the intellects could fall. So the wisdom, virtue, and freedom of Origen's intellects in their original state were not the wisdom, virtue, and freedom which the Stoic wise person enjoys. Origen's freedom in this initial state was rather the Stoic freedom we would all have enjoyed before being wise, if we had not already in the course of acquiring a will enslaved ourselves. Analogously, I argued that Origen does not believe that any misstep the intellects take turns them immediately into foolish and vicious beings, altogether deprived of freedom. After all, we would not want to say that an angel, even though he had sunk to a lower rank, was foolish, vicious, and completely enslaved. But it is this stock Stoic contrast of wisdom and folly with which Augustine operates here in the first book and repeatedly throughout all three books.

This line of thinking, for obvious reasons, gets him into great difficulties in the third book (240ff), when he tries to explain how the terrible misdeed actually came about. He is not considering just the possibility that human beings in their original state were wise in the strong sense, which creates all sorts of difficulties, as he himself sees, but also the possibility that they were like Stoic children, neither foolish nor yet wise but capable of advancing to wisdom. So Augustine at least considers replacing the stock Stoic contrast between the wise, virtuous, and free and the foolish, vicious, and unfree, as far as the first member of the pair is concerned, with a weaker though still Stoically inspired contrast between human beings not yet enslaved, but also not yet really virtuous and wise, and human beings who are foolish, vicious, and enslaved.

He is adamant about the second member of the contrasting pair. According to Augustine, as in Stoicism, this terrible deed cost us our freedom *(libertas)* altogether. We are now enslaved by our libido, by our inappropriate attachments. And, as in Stoicism, if we are not virtuous, wise, and free, nothing we can do is right. Even if we do the right thing, it will be done at least partly with the wrong motivation. It is only if we are liberated that we shall recover this freedom to act rightly and do the right thing with the right motivation (II.43).

So, according to Augustine, in our present state we are not free. We do not have a free will in the sense that we have a will which is actually free to choose. Unfortunately, this is somewhat obscured in the *De libero arbitrio* by three facts. First, the treatise is not concerned with the explanation of each and every sin we commit but rather with the proper characterization and explanation of the original misdeed which we, collectively or individually, committed and which is the source of all the evil we are born into, including our inability not to sin. It is crucial for Augustine's position that we committed this original misdeed of our own free choice. This, though, does not mean that all our sins are a matter of our free choice. They are not. Except for the original sin, they are the product of the choices of our already enslaved will. If God is not responsible for this sinning, it is because we by our first sin enslaved ourselves, and thus, even if we now cannot chose otherwise than to sin, we have brought this upon ourselves through our original sin.

Second, though Augustine does deny us freedom in our present state, the language he uses to mark the fact that we are still responsible for what we are doing is rather confusing. He talks as if the choices and decisions we make even after the fall were an exercise of our *liberum arbitrium*. And this cannot but create the impression that, even after the fall, we retain a free will. But this is not so. It is, for Augustine, one thing to have freedom *(libertas)* and hence a free will and another thing to have *liberum arbitrium* (see *CD* I.25). By the latter Augustine means that it is up to us, that it is in our power to give assent or not, that it depends on us whether or not we choose to act in a certain way. That is to say, Augustine's notion of a *liberum arbitrium* is the equivalent of the Stoic notion of something's being up to us *(eph' hēmin)*. And just as in Stoicism, so also for Augustine, the fact that we enslaved ourselves does not mean that it no longer depends on us how we choose. Hence we continue to be responsible for what we are doing, and thus to be culpable, even if now our choice is no longer free but forced. In contrast, our original wrong choice was not forced *(non cogitur,* II.200) but "voluntary" and hence deservedly subject to punishment.

Third, if we do not see the Stoic background of Augustine's position, we are going to be encouraged in the false supposition that, according to Augustine, our will is free even in the fallen state, because of his repeated remarks that our will is in our power, and that indeed nothing is as much in our power as our will (see *De lib. ar.* I.86): "We just have to will to have a good will." We need to remember, though, that this was precisely Epictetus's doctrine: we do not have a choice as to what happens in the world, but we do have a choice as to what we will, a choice as to what kind of will we want to have. This does not mean, either for Epictetus or for Augustine, that this choice we have is free.

That it does not mean this for Augustine is clear because he also explicitly tells us (II.205) that, though we were free to do what brought about our fall, we are not free to do what would bring about the restoration to our original state of freedom. Once we have fallen, we are not free to liberate ourselves. Only God can liberate us from the condition of sin into which we have fallen (II.143). Our restoration would require a complete conversion, a turning away from what we have enslaved ourselves to and a turning instead to the good, from which we had turned away in sinning. This conversion minimally requires a good will, that is to say, the will to act rightly, to do right things with the right motivation. But, according to Augustine, we are not even able without divine grace to will to have a good will once we are enslaved, though nothing is so much in our power as our will. And, needless to say, just to have the will to have a good will is not yet actually to have a good will and to have a good will is not yet to be able to do what one wills to do with the best of intentions. So even with the will to have a good will, only a beginning is made.

Augustine graphically describes this in the *Confessions* (VIII.5–9) as a battle between two wills, a new will and the old enslaved will. The only way the new will has any chance to overcome the old will is by being wholehearted, not dithering, uncompromising. But even this is not going to restore the freedom we originally enjoyed. For it will remain a constant battle for the rest of this life. It will still be the case that we have enormous difficulties in doing the right things, and even if we manage, it will not be entirely for the right reasons.

So here we do have a major difference between Augustine and Origen. It results from the fact that Augustine, like the Stoics, but unlike Origen, denies any freedom, once we have sinned. And the difference shows up in their different understandings of the passages in Paul which seem to deny us a free will, passages like *Ep. ad Rom.* 9.6 and *Ep. ad Phil.* 2.13, which ascribe both the doing and the willing to God. We saw how Origen, relying on the Stoic doctrine of a universal divine providence, was ready to accept that our actions out in the world in some sense are God's doing, because God allows us to succeed in what we are doing only if it fits in with his plan. But Origen was quite unwilling to accept Paul's claim that our willing too is God's. We saw how he tried in vain to interpret Paul as saying something which preserved the freedom of our will, if not the freedom of our actions. Augustine, however, has no difficulty in accepting the Pauline claims. His view is that even if we manage to will the right thing in our fallen state, this is so only by divine grace because God set things up in such a way that we will or want the right thing. In this sense, also for Augustine, both the doing and the willing are God's. Thus God can set things up in such a way that some of us will be led to will to have a good will, to will to free ourselves of our enslavements and to succeed in our struggles.

This is the story of Augustine's conversion in the *Confessions* (VIII.12). God made a child shout *tolle, lege! tolle, lege*; there was a copy of Paul's *Epistles* lying ready there; he opened it and read at random *Epistle to the Romans* 13:13, "No reveling or drunkenness, no debauchery or vice, no quarrels or jealousies! Let Christ Jesus himself be the armor that you wear; give no more thought to satisfying the bodily appetites." So God set things up in such a way that Augustine finally came to see that he would gain his freedom only through Christ. But, once we have forfeited our freedom, God is under no obligation to set things up in such a way as to allow us to regain it. If he does so, this is by a pure act of grace for no merit of our own, neither of our own willing nor of our own doing.

To judge Augustine's originality it is crucial to see that he differs from Origen at least in part because, unlike Origen, he follows the Stoic view that we have entirely lost our freedom. According to the Stoic position, as I explicated it before, human viciousness and folly are no impediment to God's execution of his providential plan, because the enslavement from which human beings suffer is self-inflicted. All God has to do is set things up in such a way that human beings will have the will to do what God wants them to do. Since this choice or assent is not free but enslaved, he simply has to put them into circumstances which will force their assent. So, even on this Stoic theory, both the willing and the doing in the case of the enslaved person are God's.

But we also need to keep in mind that Augustine's interpretation of Paul seems to be rather like Marius Victorinus's interpretation. Unfortunately, Victorinus's commentary on Paul's *Letter to the Romans* is lost. But we do have Victorinus's commentary on the *Letter to the Philippians* and thus on one of the passages Origen had such difficulties with (*Phil.* 2.13).[14] There Victorinus takes the position that, as Paul says, God operates in us so as to make us will what he wants us to but also arranges the world in such a way that our willing is efficacious, that is to say, that the action manages to get done. So for Victorinus already both the willing and the doing are God's. Hence, if we do something which leads to our salvation, it nevertheless has its origin in God's conditioning our will and our circumstances appropriately. Let us also note that in Augustine's account so far there is not a trace of voluntarism. It is true that we can will to have a different will and that we can will to have a good will. But this is not due to a voluntaristic conception of the will. It is due, rather, to the fact that, in the fallen state we are in, our will is no longer free but for this very reason can be made to will to have a different will, by God.

With this we can return to the "terrible deed" which lost us our freedom. How are we to explain this deed? At the end of book II of the *De libero arbitrio* Augustine claims that he does not know the answer to this question. This might be understood in various ways. It might be taken straightforwardly as a confession of ignorance concerning such dark matters. It might also be taken as an acknowledgment on Augustine's part that, given the corner he has put himself into with his conception of our original state in which our will was not enslaved, he is now unable to explain original sin. But what he means is clearly something else. He means to say that he does not know the answer, because there is nothing there to be known, to be understood. Somebody who in this original state freely chooses to act wrongly by this very act puts himself outside the intelligible, rational order of things and does something which is unintelligible, utterly irrational.

In book III.240ff, as we have seen, Augustine tries to provide an explanation for the original sin by suggesting that perhaps man was not created foolish but also not created wise, either. In this state he would have enough understanding to listen to and understand God's precepts. And in this state it would be reasonable for him to follow these precepts to gain the understanding and wisdom he does not yet have (III.244–45). Thus, on this assumption, man in the original state, if he is not yet wise, can sin in two ways. He can either fail to accept a precept or he can fail to follow it (III.246).

This suggested account now looks very much like a mixture of two Stoic theories. In part it follows the Stoic account of how children, who are not yet either wise or foolish, are raised by means of precepts whose wisdom they will only be able to understand once they themselves have acquired reason.[15] And in part it seems to be patterned on what I take to be Posidonius's account of the corruption of mankind.[16] There was a time, a golden age, when we lived happily in a state of nature and when those who were not wise were not foolish, either, but freely followed the precepts of those who were wise. At this point there was no need for a political community, for a temporal law, for coercion. But then people became corrupted, selfish, greedy, jealous, aggressive, each one looking out for what, in his lack of wisdom, he considered to be his own good rather than the common good. They no longer freely followed the wise. Hence the natural authority of the wise has been replaced by the political authority of rulers, backed up by coercive laws.

Augustine in fact suggests that the original sin may consist in man's failing to remain completely focused on, and enamored with, the Good or God, turning away from God to himself, becoming enamored with himself and concerned with his own good, in contradistinction to the Good (III.255; see also II.199). This inappropriate attachment to oneself and one's own good Augustine calls pride (*superbia*, III.263). It is the inappropriate counterpart to the desire of the spirit to respect oneself and others.

Again in all this attempt to explain original sin there is no trace of voluntarism. It is clear that in Augustine's view original sin is possible only because of a lack of wisdom, or at least a failure to exercise wisdom. There is no suggestion that the original sin consisted of disobedience to God's precepts or commands, because one has to obey God's commands, whatever they may be, by a sheer act of the will. To the contrary, it clearly is also Augustine's view that, if the original sin consisted of an act of disobedience, what was sinful about it was that it is singularly unwise not to follow the precepts of God, who is wise and good, so long as one has not acquired the wisdom to see for oneself that this is how one should behave.

On the whole, then, it does seem to me that Augustine's account differs markedly from Origen's, mainly by being much closer to Stoicism in its doctrine of freedom than Origen's account was. This allows Augustine also to follow Paul much more closely along lines already suggested by Marcus Victorinus. But it also saddles Augustine with an account of the original sin which seems much less satisfactory than Origen's and which creates tensions in various regards which threaten to make the account, if not unintelligible, then at least rather implausible and artificial.

Whatever we think of the merits of Augustine's account, it does not rely on a new notion of free will. It rather relies very extensively on the Stoic notion of a free will, and correspondingly of an enslaved will, and on how in the Stoic universe God makes use of the enslaved will to direct the course of events providentially, except that in Augustine this turns into a doctrine of grace for those who benefit from God's predetermination.

CHAPTER TEN

Conclusion

We set out to inquire, first, when people started to think of human beings as having a free will; second, what was involved in thinking of human beings in this way; and, third, why one found this way of thinking about human beings helpful. But we also raised a fourth question, whether this notion of a free will, however helpful one may have found it in late antiquity, was basically flawed right from the beginning. We have tried to give an answer to the first three questions.

The notion of a free will first arises in late Stoicism in the first century A.D. It is a notion we clearly find in Epictetus.

The notion is the conception of an ability to make choices and decisions, in particular choices and decisions which amount to one's willing to do something. And this ability is supposed to be potentially or actually free in the sense that, if it actually is free, there is nothing in the world, no force or power in the world outside us which can prevent us in virtue of this ability from making the choices or decisions we need to make to attain a good life. It is an ability which at least is potentially free in the sense that one in principle can attain this freedom. Whether we have a will which actually is free depends on our not enslaving ourselves to the world and in this way giving the world, and the powers and forces which govern the world, power over us, power even over our choices and decisions.

The notion was regarded as helpful, because there was a widespread but vague fear, especially as antiquity advanced, to put it in Plotinus's terms, that "we might be nothing" (*mē pote ouden esmen, Enn.* VI.8.1.26–27) and ultimately have no control whatsoever over our life. This fear was fed by the belief that one lived in a world full of forces and powers, many, if not most, of them hidden from us, which seemed to leave little or no room for the free pursuit of our own interests. These were either blind forces or forces which pursued their own interests without regard to us or downright hostile and malicious forces, out to tyrannize, enslave, or seduce us. The Stoics themselves had greatly contributed to giving some respectability to such fears by developing a theory that everything which happens in the world, including our actions, happens according to a divine providential plan. So it seemed particularly incumbent upon the Stoics to explain how such a seamless divine providential order was compatible with human choices. They tried to do this with their doctrine of freedom and a free will.

Platonists and Peripatetics adopted notions of a will, of freedom, and of a free will suitably modified to fit their theories. But those who were particularly eager to adopt a doctrine of a free will were the Christians. I have tried to explain why this was so. They shared with the Stoics the view that the world down to the smallest detail is governed by a divine providential order. So they too had to explain how this left any room for human freedom. But, more important, they were confronted, often within their own ranks, with theories that the order of the world we live in cannot be due to God, precisely because it systematically prevents many of us from attaining a good life, whereas others cannot fail to attain a good life.

We found that in answer to such views the Christians by no means developed a distinctive doctrine of a free will of their own, let alone a radically new view. They largely relied on the Stoic view. And whereas Origen had a position which differed from the Stoic view quite significantly, in that he assumed all human beings to be actually free and able to retain a degree of freedom, Augustine turns out to differ from Origen, not by moving further away from Stoicism but by adhering to it much more closely than Origen did. In part Augustine may have chosen this path under the influence of Paul. It nevertheless was the Stoic position to deny us, as long as we are not free, a willing of our own, as opposed to a willing by grace. This, given Augustine's influence, had enormous consequences for doctrinal development in the West. We would get a measure of this if we looked at John of Damascus at the turn from the seventh to the eighth century in the East; John has a lot to say about the will, but he has moved far away from Stoicism and relies on a Platonist view enriched by a good dose of Aristotle's ethics.[1]

Instead of turning to the enormous historical consequences of Augustine's position, I want, at least briefly, to address the last question we raised initially: "Was the notion of a free will flawed from its very beginning?" The answer seems to me to be negative in the following sense.

Of all the major ancient philosophers we have come across, only Alexander of Aphrodisias lets himself be driven into accepting a conception of a free will which is very close to the kind of conception criticized nowadays by philosophers. All the other authors we have considered seem to me to have notions of a free will which, perhaps for good reasons, we might not want to accept but which do not seem to be basically flawed in the way a notion like Alexander's is. To the contrary, considered from a sufficiently abstract level and disregarding the particular features which reflect their particular historical circumstances, they seem to me to more or less share one feature which I find rather attractive. They all involve the idea that to have a good life one must be able to make the choices one needs to make in order to have such a life. They also involve the idea that what prevents one from making these choices is that one forms false beliefs or irrational attachments and aversions which are in conflict with the choices one would have to make. Given these false beliefs and inappropriate attachments or aversions, one is not free to make the choices one would reasonably want to make. So, to be free, to have a free will, we have to liberate ourselves from these false beliefs and from attachments and aversions which are not grounded in reality. We can do this, moreover, because the world does not systematically force these beliefs, attachments, and aversions on us.

This does not seem to me to be a basically flawed idea at all, but also, without being developed appropriately, it is not much of an idea. Explaining that, however, is not a task for a historian.

ABBREVIATIONS

Acad.	Cicero, *Academica*
Adv. haer.	Irenaeus, *Adversus haereses*
ANRW	*Aufstieg und Niedergang der römischen Welt*
CC	Origen, *Contra Celsum*
CD	Augustine, *De civitate Dei*
Conf.	Augustine, *Confessions*
De an.	Aristotle, *De anima*
De lib. ar.	Augustine, *De libero arbitrio*
De princ.	Origen, *De principiis*
DL	Diogenes Laertius, *Lives and Doctrines of Eminent Philosophers*
EN	Aristotle, *Nicomachean Ethics*
Enn.	Plotinus, *Enneads*
Ep.	Seneca, *Epistulae morales*
Fat.	Alexander of Aphrodisias, *De fato*
HE	Eusebius, *Ecclesiastical History*
PE	Eusebius, *Praeparatio Evangelica*
LS	A. A. Long and D. N. Sedley, *The Hellenistic Philosophers* (Cambridge, 1987)
PG	*Patrologia Graeca*

Phd.	Plato, *Phaedo*
PHP	Galen, *On the Doctrines of Plato and Hippocrates*
Rep.	Plato, *Republic*
Retr.	Augustine, *Retractiones*
Tim.	Plato, *Timaeus*
Stob., *Ecl.*	Stobaeus, *Eclogae*
SVF	*Stoicorum Veterum Fragmenta,* ed. H. von Arnim (Leipzig, 1903–1905)
VP	Porphyry, *Vita Platonis*

NOTES

Occasionally, where Frede's point in his typescript was clearly an annotation or parenthetical, I have transferred the passage to a note. However, most of these notes are mine and are designated as such by the angle brackets (<...>) that introduce and end them.

CHAPTER I. INTRODUCTION

1. <W. D. Ross, *Aristotle* (London, 1923), 201.>

2. <In chapter 3 of The Concept of Mind (London, 1949) Ryle undertakes to refute not only the notion of a free will but, first and foremost, the notion that there exists any mental faculty of the will. Bernard Williams, in chap. 2 of *Shame and Necessity* (1993; repr., Berkeley 2008), argues that the absence of the "will" from Homer's epics should be applauded rather than regretted. Williams's book is based on the lectures he gave at Berkeley as Sather Professor in 1989.>

3. <Frede's typescript says, "Dihle calls it 'our notion of the will,'" but I have not found that exact phrase in Dihle's book. On the last page of his book's main text, Dihle writes: "St. Augustine was, in fact, the inventor of our modern notion of will." (Dihle, *The Theory of Will in Classical Antiquity* [Berkeley, 1982], 144). For further discussion and criticism of Dihle, see C. H. Kahn, "Discovering the Will: From Aristo-

tle to Augustine," in J. M. Dillon and A. A. Long, eds., *The Question of "Eclecticism": Studies in Later Greek Philosophy* (Berkeley, Calif., 1988), 236–38, and J. Mansfeld, "The Idea of the Will in Chrysippus, Posidonius, and Galen," *Proceedings of the Boston Area Colloquium in Ancient Philosophy* 7 (1991): 108–10.>

4. <I think Frede is right to take much of Dihle's discussion of "will" to be about "a notion of a free will," though Dihle does not say this in so many words. Rather than speaking of "free will," he tends to refer to "pure will" or "sheer volition" or "clear-cut notion of will." Frede's reading, however, is strongly supported by what Dihle writes at the end of his chapter "The Greek View of Human Action I": "Free will does not exist in its own right [in the Greek view] as it does according to St. Augustine's anthropology" (*Theory of Will*, 45).>

5. <Pages in Dihle's *Theory of Will* that Frede may have had in mind include 15–16, 51, 63–65, 134–35, and, esp., 20: "The word 'will' . . . as applied to the description and evaluation of human action denotes sheer volition, regardless of its origin in either cognition or emotion." Dihle is primarily interested in arguing that early Christian theologians developed a new psychology and anthropology in order to register a person's individual commitment to God.>

6. <For the use in Gnostic texts of the word *archontes,* see R. A. Bullard and B. Layton, "The Hypostasis of the Archons," in J. M. Robinson, ed., *The Nag Hammadi Library in English* (San Francisco, 1988), 161–69. Frede expands his treatment of Gnostic powers in chap. 7, p. 114.>

7. <Frede was probably thinking of Epicurus, *Letter to Menoeceus,* 134.>

8. <The planets were so named in Greek because they were popularly thought to wander. The "extreme regularity" (perfect circularity) of planetary motions was a special cosmological theory that corrected their erratic positions as perceived by the naked eye.>

9. <The main evidence concerning this swerve comes from Lucretius (*De rerum natura* 2.225–93), who is generally assumed to depend on the lost words of Epicurus.>

10. <For the evidence and discussion, see S. Bobzien, *Determinism and Freedom in Stoic Philosophy* (Oxford, 1998).>

11. <For the identity of God and fate in Stoicism, see DL 7.135 (LS 46B).>

12. <Alexander of Aphrodisias makes this argument in *On Fate.*>

13. <I have substituted the words "irrespective of the fact that" for Frede's typescript, which begins a new sentence after "raise our arm" with the words "It is not just that the world out there.">

CHAPTER 2. ARISTOTLE ON CHOICE WITHOUT A WILL

1. <See Plato, *Rep.* 8, 577e, ps.- Plato, *Definitions* 413c8; Aristotle, *EN* 3, 1113a15–b2; *EN 5*, 1136b6–7.>

2. <See Plato, *Rep.* 4, 439a–441c, and Aristotle, *EN* 1,1102b13–1103a3.>

3. <Frede refers to comments on Socrates by Aristotle, *EN* 7, 1145b23–27, 1147b13–19.>

4. <Aristotle, *EN* 7, 1145b21–1146b5.>

5. <Ibid., 1148a9.>

6. Ibid., 3, 1110b18–1111a21. Conventional translations are "of one's own accord," "on purpose," "deliberately," "willingly," "intentionally," and the converse.>

7. <Frede was probably thinking of Cicero, *Acad.* 1.40, where Cicero describes the Stoic Zeno's doctrine that assent is *in nobis et voluntariam* (in us and voluntary).>

8. <For further discussion see A. Kenny, *Aristotle's Theory of the Will* (New Haven, Conn., 1979); C.H. Kahn, "Discovering the Will: From Aristotle to Augustine," in J.M. Dillon and A.A. Long, eds., *The Question of "Eclecticism": Studies in Later Greek Philosophy* (Berkeley, Calif.), 239–41; and S. Broadie, "The Voluntary," chap. 3, in *Ethics with Aristotle* (Oxford, 1991). >

9. <Aristotle principally discusses *prohairesis* in *EN* 3, 1111b5–1113a33, and 6, 1139a31–b13.>

10. <Aristotle, *EN* 3, 1111b29–30.>

11. <Ibid., 3, 1112b11–24.>

12. <See Aristotle, *Metaphysics* 12, 7–9, with commentary in M. Frede and D. Charles, eds., *Aristotle's "Metaphysics" Lambda: Symposium Aristotelicum* (Oxford, 2000).>

CHAPTER 3. THE EMERGENCE OF A NOTION
OF WILL IN STOICISM

1. <Evidence on Stoic psychology, physiology, and ethics, to which Frede refers in the first pages of this chapter, is translated and discussed in LS 39, 58, 60, 61, 63, and 65. For detailed treatments see M. Frede, "The Stoic Conception of Reason," in K.J. Boudouris, ed., *Hellenistic Philosophy* (Athens, 1994), 2:50–63, and "The Stoic Doctrine of the Affections of the Soul," in M. Schofield and G. Striker, eds., *The Norms of Nature* (Cambridge, 1986), 93–112; B. Inwood, *Ethics and Human Action in Early Stoicism* (Oxford, 1985), chaps. 2 and 3; and A.A. Long, *Stoic Studies* (Berkeley, Calif., 1996), chaps. 10 and 12.>

2. <*Prot.* 352b–c.>

3. <For Stoic use of the term, see DL 7.159 and Aetius 4.21.1–4 (LS 53H).>

4. <See Plutarch, *De virtute morali* 441c–d (LS 61B, 9–11).>

5. <To fit Aristotelian doctrine, I take Frede's statement about the "growth of reason" to refer not to the origin of human rational capacity but to the postnatal development of reasoning; see *Metaphysics* 1.1, 980a29–b13; and *Posterior Analytics* 1.1 and 2.19. Thanks to Alan Code and Dorothea Frede for discussion of this point.>

6. <See p. 21.>

7. <Essential evidence in LS 39E, 53B, 57A. For discussion that amplifies the points made here, see Frede, "Stoic Conception of Reason," 50–53, and Frede's essay "On the Stoic Conception of the Good," in K. Ierodiakonou, ed., *Topics in Stoic Philosophy* (Oxford, 1999), 73–75.>

8. <Evidence on Stoic "impressions" is translated and discussed in LS 39. Frede's treatment of the theory here can be supplemented with his essay "Stoics and Skeptics on Clear and Distinct Impressions," in M. Burnyeat, ed., *The Skeptical Tradition* (Berkeley, Calif., 1983), 65–93, also published as chap. 9 in Frede's *Essays in Ancient Philosophy* (Minneapolis, Minn., 1987).>

9. <For the term see Stobaeus, *Ecl.* 2.86–87 (*SVF* 3. 169), and Epictetus 1.1.12, and for discussion see Inwood, *Ethics and Human Action,* 55–63.>

10. <DL 7.51 (LS 39A).>

11. <*SVF* i. 58. >

12. <DL 7.50 (LS 39G) and Sextus Empiricus, *Adversus mathematicos* 7. 229–31. According to these sources, Chrysippus was objecting to a literal interpretation of the term *impression,* which would exclude the mind from experiencing a *modification* (his preferred term), consisting of representation of multiple objects at the same time.>

13. <Frede is certainly right to attribute the idea of "incipient passion" to later Stoics, but the actual term, *propatheia,* is first connected with this idea by Philo of Alexandria and thereafter by Origen and Jerome. See M. Graver, "Philo of Alexandria and the Origin of the Stoic προπάθειαι," *Phronesis* 44 (1999): 300–25.>

14. <The Stoics called the emotional responses of the wise man *eupatheiai,* "good feelings" (DL 7.116 [LS 55F]).>

15. <Aristotle too calls acting not under compulsion or ignorance *hekōn* (*EN* 3, 1111a22–24), as Frede says on p. 24, but in Frede's interpretation the term there lacks the voluntarist connotations it will acquire later.>

16. <DL 7.115. > This distinction should not obscure the fact (which is not apparent when one, for instance, reads Stobaeus, *Ecl.* II, 87, 14ff in isolation) that for the Stoics all appetites are also willings.

17. <See, for instance, 1.4.18–21, 1.17.21–28, 2.2.1–7, 3.5.3, 3.6.4, 3.9.11. Discussions of Epictetus's concept of *prohairesis* include C. H. Kahn, "Discovering the Will: From Aristotle to Augustine," in J. M. Dillon and A. A. Long, eds., *The Question of "Eclecticism": Studies in Later Greek Philosophy* (Berkeley, Calif., 1988), 251–55; R. Dobbin, "Prohairesis in Epictetus," *Ancient Philosophy* 11 (1991): 111–35; A. A. Long, *Epictetus: A Stoic and Socratic Guide to Life* (Oxford, 2002), chap. 8; and R. Sorabji, *Self* (Oxford, 2006), chap. 10.>

18. <This is the topic of Epictetus 1.1. For extensive discussion, see S. Bobzien, *Determinism and Freedom in Stoic Philosophy* (Oxford, 1998), chap. 7.>

19. <I have added *particular* before *choice* in this sentence and *freely* in the next sentence, in the belief that these additions may clarify Frede's intended points.>

CHAPTER 4. LATER PLATONIST AND
PERIPATETIC CONTRIBUTIONS

1. <See *EN* 6, 1141a27–28. I have added the words "some of them, according to him.">

2. I have deleted the following paragraph because it seems intrusive: "In fact, if we look at Plato's division of the soul in the *Republic*, though the argument for it is based on the assumption that there can be conflicts of desire which can only be explained in terms of different parts of the soul as the subjects of these desires, it turns out that the conflict is as much a conflict of desires as it is a conflict of <what the Stoics call> impressions *(phantasiai)* or even beliefs *(doxai)*."

3. <For instance, Nemesius, *De natura hominis* 291, 1–8 (LS 53O) and, much more fully, Alexander of Aphodisias, *Fat.* 182, 16–183, 24.>

4. <See L. Edelstein and I. G. Kidd, eds., *Posidonius* (Cambridge, 1972), 1:F157–69.>

5. <See J. Cooper, "Posidonius on Emotions," in *Reason and Emotion* (Princeton, 1999).>

6. <See DL 7.89 with other texts cited at *SVF* 3.228–36, and I. G. Kidd, "Posidonius on Emotions," in A. A. Long, ed., *Problems in Stoicism* (London, 1971), 206–207.>

7. <See Seneca, *Ep.* 90.>

8. <The words "in some sense, outside us" are obscure in grammar and sense. I take Frede to mean that, in the position Posidonius contested, our impressions "originate in reasons' beliefs, and thus" are "ultimately" the result "in some sense" of factors "outside us," namely, the mistaken beliefs of society.>

9. <If Frede was thinking of Seneca, *De ira* 2.1.1–2.3.5, as is probable, his observation about Seneca's systematically ambiguous use of terms for emotions is hardly borne out by the Latin text. In fact, Seneca is at great pains to distinguish involuntary impressions or impulses from anger, which requires the mind's voluntary assent. However, his discussion is sometimes loose and more rhetorical than consistent; see M. Graver, *Stoicism and Emotion* (Chicago, 2007), chap. 4.>

10. <The best Greek evidence for Frede's point is Epictetus (though he does not use the term *propatheia*), as cited by Aulus Gellius 19.1.14–21.>

11. <I have inserted *not*.>

12. <For Longinus, see L. Brisson and M. Patillon in *ANRW* II 36, no. 1 (1994): 5214–99, and for Numenius, M. Frede, *ANRW* II 36, no. 2 (1987): 1034–75.>

13. <Frede did not give any reference to Plotinus. I have found just one instance in the *Enneads* of the Stoic term for assent *(synkatathesis)*, at *Enn.* 1.8.14.>

14. <Frede did not complete his reference to Aspasius. I asked Robert Sharples if he could supply some appropriate passage(s), to which he replied: "The problem here is that one doesn't (I think) find Aspasius saying precisely this (if one did, much of the scholarly debate about the origins of the notion of will would have been less necessary); rather, it is that in paraphrasing Aristotle Aspasius changes or adds to some of the formulations (perhaps under Stoic influence) in ways that can be seen as pointing in this direction, whether or not he was aware of it. The passages have been discussed from this point of view by Antonini Alberti, 'Il volontario e la scelta in Aspasio,' in A. Alberti and R.W. Sharples, eds., *Aspasius: The Earliest Extant Commentary on Aristotle's Ethics* (Berlin, 1999), 107–41.">

15. <Frede probably had chiefly in mind the work of Evagrius (b. ca. A.D. 345) entitled *On Thoughts* (Peri logismōn). There Evagrius distinguishes between angelic, human, and demonic thoughts, taking the latter to be generated by actual demons. For discussion, including Evagrius's endorsement of the Platonic triparite division of the soul, see the introductory chapter of R.E. Sinkewicz, *Evagrius of Pontus: The Greek Ascetic Corpus* (Oxford, 2003).>

16. <I have let this sentence stand, but I have little idea of what Frede's point is.>

17. <I have added *indirectly*.>

18. <Frede refers to *Enn.* VI.8.5.35, where the Greek word is *noōthēnai*.>

CHAPTER 5. THE EMERGENCE OF A NOTION
OF A FREE WILL IN STOICISM

1. <See *EN* 3, 1110a23–26.>
2. <*SVF* 3.544.>
3. <See *SVF* 3.127–39 and LS 58EF.>
4. <I have added the words in parentheses, by way of clarification. >
5. <For evidence on this Stoic theory, see LS 53PQ. >
6. <See Cicero, *De finibus* 3.17–22 (LS 59D) and Epictetus, 1.6.12–22 (LS 63E). Frede's thoughts on rationality and goodness are amplified in his essay "On the Stoic Conception of the Good," in K. Ierodiakonou, ed., *Topics in Stoic Philosophy* (Oxford, 1999), 71–94.>
7. <Musonius, fr. 12 Hense, and Epictetus 4.1 (his discourse on freedom). For uses of the term in later writers, see S. Bobzien, *Determinism and Freedom in Stoic Philosophy* (Oxford, 1998), 355.>
8. <See p. 34.>
9. <See p. 54.>
10. <See LS 59FGIT.>
11. <See also A. A. Long, *Epictetus: A Stoic and Socratic Guide to Life* (Oxford, 2002), 221–22.>
12. <See, for instance, 1.17.28; 2.7.13; 2.16.16; 1.17.22; 2.19.24.>
13. <See LS 62CD.>
14. <For the evidence and its interpretation, see Bobzien, *Determinism and Freedom*, 112–16.>
15. <Frede's reference to these "three" factors indicates that he must have had some quite specific text or texts in mind. His three "crucial factors" precisely match the first three personae Cicero enumerates in *De officiis* 1.107–16, which are generally taken to be derived from the Stoic Panaetius (late second century B.C.). Epictetus may well have been influenced by this scheme, but, if so, his deployment of it is more fluid: cf. Long, *Epictetus*, 256–57.>
16. <*Politics* 1.5.>
17. <*Metaphysics* 12, 1075a11–24.>
18. This is why Aristotle answers the general question "What is the right thing to do?" not by giving us a list, like the decalogue, but by saying what "the practically wise man" would do.

CHAPTER 6. PLATONIST AND PERIPATETIC CRITICISMS AND RESPONSES

1. <For further discussion, see A.A. Long, *Hellenistic Philosophy: Stoic, Epicureans, Sceptics,* 2d ed. (Berkeley, Calif., 1986), 101–104, and R.J. Hankinson, "Determinism and Indeterminism," in K. Algra et al., eds., *The Cambridge History of Hellenistic Philosophy* (Cambridge, 1999), 519–22, 529–34.>

2. It seems entirely reasonable to say that there are certain things that we naturally will or want and that it is our nature to will or want certain things, like food and drink or, for that matter, a good life. This idea will later play a prominent role in Maximus Confessor and in John of Damascus in their rejection of monotheletism, that is, the view that Jesus Christ has two natures but only one will. They will argue that Christ as God and Christ as man have two wills, both natural wills (i.e., wills in virtue of which one wills or wants what it is one's nature to want) but that Christ, unlike other human beings, does not have a *gnomic* will, that is, his own judgment as to what he wills or does not will, which goes beyond, or even counter to, what one, given one's nature, naturally wills or wants. This creates the impression that there is just one will in Christ, since the natural human will naturally goes along with the natural divine will. <See A. Dihle, *The Theory of Will in Classical Antiquity* (Berkeley, Calif., 1982), 243 n. 112.>

3. <I omit the following two sentences in Frede's typescript: "After all, we are not just hungry and want something to eat, if there is something to eat in sight which could arouse our interest. But he also does something else.">

4. <For Alexander's text, translation, and commentary, see R.W. Sharples, *Alexander of Aphrodisias on Fate* (London, 1983).>

5. <I omit the following sentences in Frede's typescript: "Alexander, who explicitly sets out to reject universal determinism, follows Aristotle. So, according to Alexander, we determine whether we do something or not, whether this gets done or not. Alexander, not believing in universal divine providence, has no difficulty in claiming this.">

6. <This text is included in Sharples's edition of Alexander.>

7. <I consulted Robert Sharples about Frede's reference here to

Alexander's *De fato*. Sharples responded: "The passage Frede cites refers to the Stoic claim rather than to Alexander's denial of it. The problem is that Alexander doesn't, I think, explicitly claim in so many words that 'under identical conditions, both internal and external . . . it is still possible to choose and to act otherwise.' Rather, the way he formulates the case against which he is arguing shows (though not to everyone's satisfaction) that this is what he himself wants to claim." See *De fato* 190, 8; 206, 22; 207, 27, cited by Sharples, *Alexander of Aphrodisias on Fate*, 21, where he says that Alexander "objects not just to determination of our actions by external causes alone, but to that resulting from a combination of internal and external factors.">

8. <Frede does not give any page reference to Dihle. I take him to have in mind, for instance, "the idea of pure volition as separate from both cognition and emotion" (Dihle, *Theory of Will*, 135).>

CHAPTER 7. AN EARLY CHRISTIAN VIEW ON A FREE WILL: ORIGEN

1. <II *Apology* 7.5.1; *Dialogue* 88.5.2; 102.4.2, 4, 6; 141.1.6.>

2. <See *De principiis* III.1. The text, edited by P. Koetschau, appears in *Origenes Werke*, vol. 5 (Leipzig, 1913).>

3. <After naming Tatian, Frede's typescript has an incomplete sentence that I have omitted because I do not know how to complete it: "Who among Eastern Christian authors of Hellenic culture and Greek philosophy, pagan wisdom.">

4. <*Ad Graecos* 1.3.5–6.>

5. <At *Ad Graecos* 15.2–3–4 Tatian ascribes the view that animals have rationality to certain unnamed philosophers. If he is to be counted in their number, as Frede suggests, then his use of the term *aloga* (nonrational) to refer to animals (here and also at *Ad Graecos* 25.1–7–8) must be regarded as purely conventional. What Frede calls "a book on animals" would more literally be translated as "a book on living beings." For the reference to the book on daemons, see *Ad Graecos* 16.1–6, where Tatian says that he has "elsewhere" shown that daemons are not human souls.>

6. <See Frede, "Celsus Philosophus Platonicus," *ANRW* II 36, no. 7 (1994): 5183–5213 at 5211, with references to Origen, *CC* 4.79, 84, 88, 96, 97. Another second-century Platonist who champions the view that animals have intelligence is Plutarch, *De sollertia animalium*; see vol. 12 of the Loeb edition of Plutarch, *Moralia*. >

7. <See Justin, *Dialogue* 2.6. The literal historicity of the intellectual autobiography Justin presents here is sometimes doubted, but either way this passage is testimony to his belief that Platonism is the closest of the philosophical systems to Christianity. For Tatian's relationship with Justin, see Irenaeus, *Adv. haer.* 1.28.1.>

8. <See Eusebius, *HE* 6.10.1.>

9. <Rufinus of Aquileia (fl. fourth-century A.D.).>

10. <The source for this claim is Porphyry, as reported by Eusebius, *HE* VI.19.2–8. But Frede's use of *presumably* belies a long controversy about whether Porphyry can have gotten things quite right here: many scholars think that he might have confused two quite different Origens. M.J. Edwards thinks he has confused two different Ammonii as well; see "Ammonius, Teacher of Origen," *Journal of Ecclesiastical History* 44 (1993): 1–13.>

11. <Eusebius, *HE* VI.19.2–8.>

12. <Gregory (b. ca. A.D. 213) studied with Origen (the subject of his panegyric) in Caesarea, where he subsequently became bishop.>

13. <On Methodius (d. ca. 311), a Christian bishop and fierce opponent of Origen's doctrine of the Resurrection, see L.G. Patterson, *Methodius of Olympus: Divine Sovereignty, Human Freedom, and the Life of Christ.* (Washington, D.C., 1997).>

14. <The text is edited in the *Sources Chrétiennes* series by E. Junod (Paris, 1976).>

15. <Frede's Origen reference should seemingly read *Commentary on John* 32.16, 451.30–32, in E. Preuschen, ed., *Origenes Werke,* vol. 4 (Leipzig, 1903).>

16. <*De princ.* II.9.6, esp. 169.25–170.2 Koetschau. See G.R. Boys-Stones, "Human Autonomy and Divine Revelation in Origen," in S. Swain, S. Harrison, and J. Elsner, eds., *Severan Culture* (Cambridge, 2007), 488–99.>

17. <On the impossibility of direct cognizance of God (the Father), see *De princ.* I.1.5. Frede's comparison of Origen's God with Plato's Form of the Good is encouraged by the image of the sun used by both Origen and Plato in this context, as well as the consideration that contemporary Platonists regularly identified the Form of the Good with their creator god.>

18. <Origen in the *De princ.* consistently talks as if *withdrawal* from God is the only intellectual direction that the intellects (other than Christ's soul) could take, if they change at all (e.g., II.9.2). The proposal that intellects might in their prelapsarian state *advance* in knowledge more or less, even while maintaining equality with each other, is a distinctive feature of Frede's account.>

19. <Origen is actually careful to distinguish the idea that intellects are created "after the image of God" *(kat' eikona theou)*, that is, in imitation of Christ, who is the image of God: *De princ.* I.2.6; II.6.3–6; *Commentary on John* 1.17 (104–105), 22.20–26 Preuschen), from the idea of "likeness" to God *(homoiōsis)*, which is the reward for souls (understood as those same intellects in their fallen state) when they achieve restoration to their original condition. See, on this distinction especially, *De princ.* III.6.1 and *CC* 4.30, and further H. Crouzel, *Théologie de l'image de Dieu chez Origène* (Paris, 1956) (esp. pt. II, chap. 3). It is a distinction that Frede does not observe here, but perhaps his point does not require him to. After all, on any account, intellects in their original state are crucially thought of as *freely* maintaining their union with Christ (i.e., fully realizing their nature as creatures made "after the image of God") just as souls, later on, *freely* choose the path that will lead them back to this union (which is when they will achieve "likeness to God" as well). The continuity between these two phases of activity is all the more evident if one accepts Frede's proposal that intellects are created in the first place to progress in knowledge and understanding.>

20. <See esp. *De princ.* II.1.1.>

21. <For example, H. Koch, *Pronoia und Paideusis. Studien über Origenes und sein Verhältnis zum Platonismus* (Berlin, 1932), 251–53.>

22. <For both criticism and reply, see Eusebius, *Contra Marcellum*, 1.4.24–27.>

23. <By other parts of *De principiis* Frede perhaps refers to I pref. 5, and for "other writings of Origen," most explicitly, see *Fragmenta in evangelium Joannis (in catenis)*, 43.7.>

24. <See I. pref. 2 (8.14 Koetschau).>

25. <For more on Valentinus, see A. Dihle, *The Theory of Will in Classical Antiquity* (Berkeley, Calif., 1982), 150–57.>

26. <See esp. *Philocalia* 23.14–16.>

27. <The *Apocryphon of John* is translated in J. M. Robinson, ed., *The Nag Hammadi Library in English* (San Francisco, 1988), 104–23.>

28. <Frede was probably referring to a newly discovered sermon published by F. Dolbeau in *Vingt-six Sermons au people d'Afrique* (Paris, 1996), 557–59. I owe this reference to James O'Donnell.>

29. <Two lengthy extracts from Book 3 of Origen's lost *Commentary on Genesis* are given at *Philocalia* 23.1–11 and 14–21 (also, in parts, at Eusebius, *PE* 6.11).>

30. Take the reference to be a dispute about the lordships and divine powers. This must refer to the *kyriotētes* and *dynameis* mentioned by Paul in *Col.* 1, 16 and in *Eph.* 1, 21, respectively, as angelic orders (see Origen, *De princ.* 1.5.1), except that the powers here are qualified as *sacrae* (*dynameis theiai,* it seems). This in turns suggests that we have here a reference to the *theotētes,* or divinities which are mentioned in conjunction with the *kyriotētes* in Irenaeus's account of the Valentinians (*Adv. haer.* 1.4.5) and also in the Gnostic *Epistula ad Rheginum* 44, 37–38, <translated in Robinson, *Nag Hammadi Library,* 52–57>, perhaps based on an interpretation of Paul in 1 Cor. 8:5; see also Clement of Alexandria, *Excerpta ex Theodoto* 43, 2. <For these Gnostic texts see B. A. Pearson, *Gnosticism, Judaism, and Egyptian Christianity* (Minneapolis, Minn., 1990).>

31. Basilides, for instance, will regard them as creations of a much inferior being, who actually falls, namely, Sophia (see Irenaeus, *Adv. haer.* 1.24.3–5).

32. <Tatian, *Ad Graecos* 7.1. >

33. <As Dihle, *Theory of Will,* 143, concludes. >

34. <See *De princ.* I.3.8 and I.4.1.>

35. <See, for example, *PG* 46, 145.44—148.2, or again at 156.30–32,

where this "restoration" to our pristine state is said to be what the doctrine of the resurrection of the body amounts to.>

36. In Rufinus's translation *satietas*; presumably, the Greek is *koros,* but see for comparison Justinian, *Epistola ad Menam,* anathema 1.

37. <*Tim.* 41ab describes created beings whose continued existence is entirely dependent on, but by the same token guaranteed by, the goodwill of the demiurge. >

CHAPTER 8. REACTIONS TO THE STOIC NOTION OF A FREE WILL: PLOTINUS

1. <Thus Dihle says, "It is generally accepted in the study of the history of philosophy that the notion of will, as it is used as a tool of analysis and description in many philosophical doctrines from the early Scholastics to Schopenhauer and Nietzsche, was invented by St. Augustine" (A. Dihle, *The Theory of Will in Classical Antiquity* [Berkeley, Calif., 1982], 123).>

2. See R. Walzer, *Galen on Jews and Christians* (Oxford, 1949), 11ff, who cites Galen, *De usu partium* XI, 14, for this contrast. <Frede discusses Galen's theology in "Galen's Theology," in J. Barnes and J. Jouanna, eds., *Galien et la Philosophie. Entretiens sur l'antiquité classique de la Fondation Hardt* (Vandoeuvres, Switz., 2003), 49: 73–129.>

3. <Dihle, *Theory of Will,* 1. >

4. <The reference is to the four-volume *Commentaries on the Medical Doctrines of Plato's Timaeus* (*Lib. Prop.* XIX 46); fragments are printed in *Corpus Medicorum Graecorum* Supp. I (1934), and controversial "new" fragments appeared in C.J. Larrain, *Galens Kommentar zu Platons Timaios* (Teubner, Stuttgart, 1992). Thanks to J.R. Hankinson for supplying this information.>

5. Ammonius, Plotinus's teacher, took this view, as would Longinus in his conservatism. <On both figures see J. Dillon, *The Middle Platonists* (London, 1977), 380–83.>

6. <On Numenius, see Dillon, *Middle Platonists,* 366–72, and M. Frede, "Numenius," *ANRW* II 36, no. 2 (1987): 1034–75.>

7. <Plato, *Tim.* 28a, 29a, 30c.>

8. <*Rep.* 6, 509b. >

9. <The main source for Numenius's treatment of Moses and the Bible is Eusebius, *PE* IX.6.9. For further discussion see M. F. Burnyeat, "Platonism in the Bible: Numenius of Apamea on *Exodus* and Eternity," in R. Salles, ed., *Metaphysics, Soul, and Ethics in Ancient Thought* (Oxford, 2005), 143–70.>

10. <The most accessible Greek text and translation are in vol. 7 of the Loeb Classical Library edition by A. H. Armstrong (Cambridge, Mass., 1988). There is a commentary on this treatise by G. Leroux, *Plotin. Traité sur la liberté de la volonté de l'Un* (Paris, 1990).>

11. Plotinus took Aristotle to task for this in *Enn.* VI. 1.

12. <Frede evidently accepts Kirchoff's emendation *tosouton* instead of *touton,* etc., in the manuscript readings.>

13. I want to note in passing here, though this again would deserve more extensive treatment, that in Plotinus's time not much distinction seems to be made between the nonrational part of the soul and the body. The state of the nonrational part of the soul seems to be taken to be largely, if not entirely, a function of the state of the body. This is a view we find in Galen but also, it seems, in Alexander of Aphrodisias. <For Galen, see *PHP* V, 464; and for Alexander, *De anima* 24.21–23, and *Mantissa* 104.28–34. Thanks to R. W. Sharples for supplying the latter references.> We shall hardly err in assuming that this is in large part the result of the influence of medicine. But we should also remember that already in Plato's *Phaedo,* 64d–65d, perception and nonrational desire are a matter of the body. In any case, if we are motivated by appetite, Plotinus takes it that something other than us, namely, our body (not to mention the external objects of desire), is deciding what we are after. <I have supplied *after* because the sense seems to require some such conclusion to the sentence.>

14. One of Plotinus's longest and most important treatises *(Enn.* II.9) is directed against the Gnostics and their demonization of the visible world.

15. <I have substituted "with its freedom qua soul something highly tenuous and qualified" for Frede's original wording ", has been intellectualized, but that its freedom is a highly tenuous and qualified freedom.">

16. <See Frede, "Monotheism and Pagan Philosophy in Later Antiquity," in M. Frede and P. Athanassiadi, eds., *Pagan Monotheism in Late Antiquity* (Oxford, 2006), 41–69.>

17. <*Against the Christians*, fr. 76 Harnack.>

18. The feminine participles in 7.12, 13, 15 go back to the feminine "the nature *(physis)* of the good" in 7.3.

19. <See Aristotle, *De an.* 3.4.>

20. Note, though, one consequence of there being no distinction in God between willing and doing: It means that God's willing in itself amounts to something's getting done. It is this that is, or should be, meant by saying that God does things by a sheer act of will; see Methodius, *De creatis 15.*

21. A. H. Armstrong, "Two Views of freedom," *Studia Patristica* 18 (1982): 397–406.

22. See *Plotinus,* trans. A. H. Armstrong, Loeb Classical Library, 7:224.

CHAPTER 9. AUGUSTINE: A RADICALLY NEW NOTION OF A FREE WILL?

1. <On Cicero and Philo, see C. Brittain, *Philo of Larissa* (Oxford, 2001).>

2. <Ambrose's Stoicism is most evident in his work *De officiis,* which was heavily influenced by Cicero's work of the same name: see Ambrose, *De officiis,* ed. I. F. Davidson (Oxford, 2001).>

3. <See *Conf.* VIII. 2.>

4. <See P. Hadot, *Marius Victorinus* (Paris, 1971).>

5. A. Dihle, *The Theory of Will in Classical Antiquity* (Berkeley, Calif., 1982),126. <In contrast with Dihle and in affinity with Frede, Gauthier argues that Augustine's notion of the will is already completely present in the Stoics. See R. A. Gauthier, introduction to *Aristote: l'ethique à Nicomache* I, 2d ed.(Louvain, Begium, 1970), 1:259. I owe this reference to C. H. Kahn, "Discovering the Will: From Aristotle to Augustine," in J. M. Dillon and A. A. Long, eds., *The Question of "Eclecticism": Studies in Later Greek Philosophy* (Berkeley, Calif., 1988), 238.>

6. <For the evidence and discussion, see *SVF* 2.70, 74, and 90, and LS chap. 40.>

7. <III.200. This reference is to G. M. Green's edition in *Corpus Scriptorum Ecclesiasticorum Latinorum* (Vienna, 1956), vol. 74, sect. VI, pt. III. For a recent study see S. Harrison, *Augustine's Way into the Will: The Theological and Philosophical Significance of* De Libero Arbitrio (Oxford, 2006).>

8. The reason for Augustine's particular concern with Manichaeism is easy to see. This religion, soon after its rise late in the third century A.D., had rapidly spread in North Africa, where Augustine himself had been strongly attracted to it for about eight years. When he wrote the *De libero arbitrio,* it had been just a few years since he had finally rejected Manichaeism. Now, after his conversion, he turns with a vengeance against the Manichaeans. By the time he had finished the *De libero arbitrio,* he had already written two treatises against his erstwhile brethren, and many more were to follow.

9. <See J. Ferguson, *Pelagius. A Historical and Theological Study* (Cambridge, 1956).>

10. The main difference is that in Augustine's case the topic was made more urgent by his earlier involvement in Manichaeism and his converting people, like his benefactor Romanianus, to it.

11. <III.198–202. For Augustine's much later insistence on his ignorance about the soul's origin, see *Retr.* 1.1.3, a reference I owe to James O'Donnell.>

12. <Frede's typescript names O'Donnell, but I have corrected the name to O'Connell, in reference to R. J. O'Connell, *The Origin of Soul in St. Augustine's Later Works* (New York, 1987). I owe this correction to James O'Donnell.>

13. <The debate was about whether, for example, "man," signifies an actual universal or common nature (realism), existing independent of particulars or minds, or, rather, a general term or concept that has no extramental correlate (nominalism). For details see N. Kretzmann, A. Kenny, and J. Pinborg, eds., *The Cambridge History of Later Medieval Philosophy* (Cambridge, 1982).>

14. <The Pauline text, in the Revised English Bible edition (Oxford, 1989), reads: "For it is God who works in you, inspiring both the

will and the deed, for his chosen purpose." Marius Victorinus is the earliest Latin commentator on the Pauline epistles.>

15. <Frede was probably thinking of Philo, *Leg. Alleg.* 1.93 (*SVF* 3.519), which is likely to be of Stoic origin. Plutarch also advocates the use of "precepts" in the education of children (*De lib. educ.* 12).>

16. <"Posidonius's account" is an allusion to Seneca, *Ep.* 90.>

CHAPTER 10. CONCLUSION

1. <See Frede's discussion in "John of Damascus on Human Action, the Will, and Human Freedom," in K. Ierodiakonou, ed., *Byzantine Philosophy and Its Ancient Sources* (Oxford, 2002), 63–96. Frede's study is outlined by Ierodiakonou as follows (11–12): "[Frede] focuses . . . in particular on his [John's] attempt to integrate a notion of a will into Aristotle's moral psychology and theory of action. The problem here is to explain why God would create human beings if they sooner or later would sin, but also to get a better grasp of the process of how we come to make a choice. According to Michael Frede, John's account of human freedom is quite novel in some ways, and this novelty had an important impact on Thomas Aquinas, and thus on the further development of thought about the will in traditional western philosophy.">

BIBLIOGRAPHY

Alberti, A., and R.W. Sharples, eds. *Aspasius: The Earliest Extant Commentary on Aristotle's Ethics.* Berlin, 1999.

Armstrong, A.H. "Two Views of Freedom." *Studia Patristica* 18 (1982): 397–406.

Bobzien, S. *Determinism and Freedom in Stoic Philosophy.* Oxford, 1998.

Boys-Stones, G. "Human Autonomy and Divine Revelation in Origen." In S. Swain, S. Harrison, and J. Elsner, eds., *Severan Culture,* 488–99. Cambridge, 2007.

Brisson, L., and M. Papillon. "Longinus." *ANRW* II 36, no. 1 (1994): 5214–99.

Brittain, C. *Philo of Larissa.* Oxford, 2001.

Broadie, S. *Ethics with Aristotle.* Oxford, 1991.

Bullard, R.A., and R. Layton. "The Hypostasis of the Archons." In J.M. Robinson, ed., *The Nag Hammadi Library in English,* 161–69. San Francisco, 1988.

Burnyeat, M. "Platonism in the Bible: Numenius of Apamea on *Exodus* and Eternity." In R. Salles, ed., *Metaphysics, Soul, and Ethics in Ancient Thought,* 143–70. Oxford, 2005.

Cooper, J. "Posidonius on Emotions." In J. Cooper, *Reason and Emotion,* 449–84. Princeton, N.J., 1999.

Crouzel, H. *Théologie de l'image de Dieu chez Origène.* Paris, 1956.

Dihle, A. *The Theory of Will in Classical Antiquity.* Berkeley, Calif., 1982.

Dillon, J. *The Middle Platonists.* London, 1977.

Dobbin, R. "Proharesis in Epictetus." *Ancient Philosophy* 11 (1991): 111–35.

Edwards, M.J. "Ammonius, Teacher of Origen." *Journal of Ecclesiastical History* 44 (1993): 1–13.

Ferguson, J. *Pelagius: A Historical and Theological Study.* Cambridge, 1956.

Frede, M. "Celsus philosophus Platonicus." *ANRW* II 36, no. 7 (1994): 5183–5213.

———. *Essays in Ancient Philosophy.* Minneapolis, Minn., 1987.

———. "Galen's Theology." In J. Barnes and J. Jouanna, eds., *Galien et la philosophie. Entretiens sur l'antiquité classique de la Fondation Hardt,* 49:73–129. Vandoeuvres, Switz., 2003.

———. "John of Damascus on Human Action, the Will, and Human Freedom." In K. Ierodiakonou, ed., *Byzantine Philosophy and Its Ancient Sources.* Oxford, 2002.

———. "Monotheism and Pagan Philosophy in Late Antiquity." In M. Frede and P. Athanassiadi, eds., *Pagan Monotheism in Late Antiquity,* 41–69. Oxford, 2006.

———. "Numenius." *ANRW* II 36, no. 2 (1987): 1034–75.

———. "On the Stoic Conception of the Good." In K. Ierodiakonou, ed., *Topics in Stoic Philosophy,* 71–94. Oxford, 1999.

———. "Origen's Treatise against Celsus." In M. Edwards and M. Goodman, eds., *Apologetics in the Roman Empire,* 131–56. Oxford, 1991.

———. "The Stoic Conception of Reason." In K.J. Boudouris, ed., *Hellenistic Philosophy,* 2:50–63. Athens, 1994.

———. "The Stoic Doctrine of the Affections of the Soul." In M. Schofield and G. Striker, eds., *The Norms of Nature,* 93–112. Cambridge, 1986.

———. "Stoics and Skeptics on Clear and Distinct Impressions." In M. Burnyeat, ed., *The Skeptical Tradition.* Berkeley, Calif., 1983.

Frede, M., and D. Charles, eds. *Aristotle's "Metaphysics" Lambda: Symposium Aristotelicum.* Oxford, 2000.

Gauthier, R. A. *Aristote: L'éthique à Nicomache* 1.1, 2d ed. Louvain, Belgium, 1970.

Graver, M. "Philo of Alexandria and the Origin of the Stoic προπάθειαι." *Phronesis* 44 (1999): 300–25.

———. *Stoicism and Emotion.* Chicago, 2007.

Hadot, P. *Marius Victorinus.* Paris, 1971.

Hankinson, R.J. "Determinism and Indeterminism." In K. Algra, J. Barnes, J. Mansfeld, and M. Schofield, eds., *The Cambridge History of Hellenistic Philosophy, 513–41.* Cambridge, 1999.

Harrison, S. *Augustine's Way into the Will: The Theological and Philosophical Significance of* De libero arbitrio. Oxford, 2006.

Inwood, B. *Ethics and Human Action in Early Stoicism.* Oxford, 1985.

Kahn, C. H. "Discovering the Will: From Aristotle to Augustine." In J. M. Dillon and A. A. Long, eds., *The Question of "Eclecticism": Studies in Later Greek Philosophy.* Berkeley, Calif., 1988.

Kenny, A. *Aristotle's Theory of the Will.* New Haven, Conn., 1979.

Kidd, I. G. "Posidonius on Emotions." In A. A. Long, ed., *Problems in Stoicism, 200–15.* 1971. Reprint, London, 1996.

Koch, H. *Pronoia und Paideusis: Studien über Origenes und sein Verhältnis zum Platonismus.* Berlin, 1932.

Kretzmann, N., A. Kenny, and J. Pinborg, eds. *The Cambridge History of Later Medieval Philosophy.* Cambridge, 1982.

Leroux, G. *Plotin. Traité sur la liberté de la volonté de l'Un.* Paris, 1990.

Long, A. A. *Epictetus: A Stoic and Socratic Guide to Life.* Oxford, 2002.

———. *Hellenistic Philosophy: Stoics, Sceptics, Epicureans,* 2d ed. Berkeley, Calif., 1986.

———. *Stoic Studies.* Berkeley, Calif., 1996.

Long, A. A., and D. N. Sedley. *The Hellenistic Philosophers.* Cambridge, 1987.

Mansfeld, J. "The Idea of the Will in Chrysippus, Posidonius, and Galen." In *Proceedings of the Boston Area in Ancient Philosophy* 7 (1991): 107–57.

O'Connell, R. J. *The Origin of Soul in St. Augustine's Later Works.* New York, 1987.

Patterson, L. G. *Methodius of Olympus: Divine Sovereignty, Human Freedom, and the Life of Christ.* Washington, D.C., 1997.

Pearson, B. A. *Gnosticism, Judaism, and Egyptian Christianity.* Minneapolis, Minn., 1990.

Robinson, J. M., ed. *The Nag Hammadi Library in English.* San Francisco, 1988.

Ross, W. D. *Aristotle.* London, 1923.

Ryle, G. *The Concept of Mind.* London, 1949.

Sharples, R. W., ed. *Alexander of Aphrodisias on Fate.* London, 1983.

Sinkewicz, R. E. *Evagrius of Pontus: The Greek Ascetic Corpus.* Oxford, 2003.

Sorabji, R. *Self.* Oxford, 2006.

Walzer, R. *Galen on Jews and Christians.* Oxford, 1949.

Williams, B. *Shame and Necessity.* Berkeley, 1993. Reprint with a new foreword by A. A. Long, Berkeley, 2008.

INDEX

akrasia, 22–3, 29, 32, 52, 57
Alexander of Aphrodisias, 15, 57,
 58, 91, 95–101, 107, 121, 134–35, 142,
 143, 177–78
Ambrose, 155
Ammonius Saccas, 105, 194n5
animal behavior, 16, 25, 33–36,
 50–51, 53, 57, 74, 98
Aquinas, Thomas, 53
archontes, 11, 161
Aristotelians, 48–49, 52, 55, 57–58,
 74, 89, 103, 132, 157–58, 176
Aristotle, 2–5, 19–35, 42, 45–46,
 49–52, 57, 58, 61, 67–68, 72, 86, 87,
 94, 97, 98, 109, 115, 127, 133, 136, 139,
 145, 147, 150, 153, 156–57
Armstrong, A.H., 150–51
assent, 36–37, 40–48, 49, 52–53, 56,
 57–58, 60, 62, 80–82, 91, 93–97,
 108, 110, 112, 123, 158, 168, 171
Augustine, 10, 64–65, 114, 122,
 153–74, 177
autexousion, 74–75, 96, 102, 104, 113, 121

Basilides, 116, 118, 193n31

Basil of Caesarea, 106, 115
belief, 12, 20–23, 26, 32–33, 38–41, 43,
 47–48, 49–51, 54–55, 59, 75, 83, 87,
 136, 157, 158–59, 178
boulēsis, 8, 19, 42–43, 46

Calcidius, 58
Carneades, 91–95
Celsus, 104
choice, 7–9, 14, 17, 23–31, 45–48, 50,
 57, 62, 65, 76, 85, 87–88, 94, 100,
 108, 123, 128, 140, 149, 158, 161–62,
 167, 175–76, 178
Christianity, 3, 10, 18, 19, 74, 89, 102–
 8, 113–18, 120, 122, 124, 125–30, 143–
 44, 145, 150–51, 153–56, 176–77
Chrysippus, 38, 46, 53, 81–82, 90, 93,
 95, 98, 121
Cicero, 25, 37, 91, 154
Clement of Alexandria, 104
conflict of desires, 22–24, 42, 59
Cooper, J., 53

daemons, 17, 63–65, 104, 110, 121–22
Damascius, 111

203

Text:	10.75/15 Janson
Display:	Janson MT Pro
Compositor:	BookMatters, Berkeley
Printer and binder:	Sheridan Books, Inc.